"In your hands is a experience. Michael Liven journey in the realm of the Spirit of Fire and Michael's reflections and insights will ring true to those who desire to live there."
--*Tony Collis, Pastor, Hope Centre Levin, NZ*

"When I first heard that Michael Livengood had been sent to New Zealand because there were not enough experienced evangelists in New Zealand I was a bit taken back and tempted to offense, but having read Michael's latest book I now understand something of what God was doing.

Here is a practical down to earth guide to the basics that one needs to know about the wonder and pitfalls of Revival from one who has been there and done that for many years. This is the kind of hands-on experience that not many of us have and that many of us are going to need in the days to come as the Holy Spirit moves up this country in power in the near future.

I am sure that when the anointing gets overwhelming, I will be sending Air New Zealand tickets to the Hutt valley for Michael and Linda's use, and their book will be a sure and safe guide in the coming rapids of revival."
--*Rev John Cromarty, St David's On Regent, Invercargill, Evangelist*

"As I have been reading through The Wow Factor and taking notes on the words Evangelist Mike Livengood has written, I realize the outcome of revival is much more positive than the critical observations. I want to encourage anyone who desires to be in or lead a revival movement to read this book. If you are in a revival movement, this book will help you sustain the move of God. If you are skeptical, even critical of revival, this book offers strong Biblical evidence along with testimonies of experiences that support the importance of revival.

Evangelist Livengood offers extremely powerful and practical teaching on the reality of what revival really is. I am impressed with the modeling of the five-fold ministries functioning together. I would borrow a thought from Dr. Carolyn Tennant, just as the Trinity bows down to each other in honor, one never disrespecting the other, so the five-fold ministries yield to one another. Revival is neither a one-person show nor a one gift show.

My life has been transformed by the manifest presence of God. This book promotes that kind of experience with practical guidelines to experience and sustain the move of God."
--*Donald Gifford, Indiana District Assemblies of God, District Superintendent*

"Michael's book stirs up faith to believe that you and your church can experience a true move of God. Filled with practical teaching, spiritual insight, and Biblical truths, Michael helps us to believe that God wants us to experience what we believe to be elusive. I would encourage every pastor to use this book to teach their congregation about revival! In fact, the third key to revival presented in this book will be preached by every pastor who reads this book. That alone is worth purchasing this book. This book, like Michael, is practical, Pentecostal and pure!"
--*Phil Schneider, Illinois District Assemblies of God, District Superintendent*

"Over the years I have read many accounts of the remarkable things God did in people's lives during times of revival. However, this study of church revivals by Michael Livengood goes much further into this subject than anything else I have seen. Michael, himself, as a seasoned evangelist has been uniquely involved in leadership with others in a number of revivals both in the United States and in New Zealand during the past twenty or so years. From this, he has analyzed all aspects of the subject, from how revivals come about, what characterizes them and the impact they make on those who lead and benefit from them. Adding to the absorbing interest of the stories he tells is his ability to probe beyond the what to the why to focus on God's purpose in bringing revival to hungry hearts. His recorded interviews with church leaders who have been used by the Lord in revival in their own churches will be particularly helpful to all who also hunger to see God at work in their own situations. Nor does Michael shrink from discussing the things that have derailed revivals from time to time. This book, like its author, is REAL. It is a MUST for the church in the 21st century. I recommend it highly."

--Ian Clark MA, Former Principal, Assemblies of God Bible College, New Zealand

"In this book, "The Wow Factor," the author Michael Livengood makes a statement that in my opinion clarifies the age-old question… "What is Revival?" He states; "Revival is a Journey rather than An Event." Having ministered alongside Linda and Michael on many occasions over the past seven-plus years, especially at the Cross Tabernacle Outpouring in Terre Haute, Indiana I have come to know Michael as the "Noah Webster of Outpouring." The Outpouring in Terre Haute was not just another Revival. It was and still is a Journey. When this revival began, God placed men at the helm who were not only familiar with revival but had experienced in their own ministries what it was to be in extended revival meetings that would last several weeks and in some cases months. But, in Terre Haute, God took our theology of revival and threw it in the trash can! God was doing a new thing. He was taking us on a Journey that continues to this day!

As we began this Acts chapter two Outpouring Journey, God began to take us down a path we had never traveled before as He took control of the service and began introducing us to the working of the Holy Spirit through the Five-Fold ministry. Oftentimes, after two hours of ministry where people got saved, healed, delivered and ministered to by Word of Knowledge or Prophecy, we would sit there and ask the question… "What Just Happened?" Michael would come to the podium and under the anointing of the Holy Spirit would in the simplest of layman's terms, using the Word of God define exactly what had just taken place and what we could expect as a result of what God had just done.

Every Pastor, Evangelist, and Layperson who is hungering for an Outpouring of Revival in their church or where they are being sent to minister needs to read this book! Every church that is experiencing an Outpouring Revival and wants to know how to sustain such a move of the Holy Spirit needs to read this Book! This book is a God Inspired Manual on an Acts chapter two Outpouring.

In this book, the Author will take you on a Journey answering the question, how do we attain revival? Once we have attained revival, how do we sustain revival? What are the 5 stages of Revival, and how do these stages build on one another? It is in "Stage One" that you learn the Wow Factor that focuses on who Christ is, and in "Stage Two" you learn the Wow Factor that focuses on the Wow of His Power. If you want to know what stage 3-5 are, you need to read the book!

With direction that only comes from the Throne, Michael lists in this book the 5 Keys to Revival. Interestingly enough, Prayer is not one of the keys but is a result of Key number one. O' you must read this book!!!

One of the greatest questions asked by those who are experiencing an Outpouring Revival is; how do I go about pastoring this Move of God? How do I sustain it? What are some of the pitfalls? Will all my church embrace it once they experience it?

To answer these questions, Michael enlists the help of five Pastors whose churches have been experiencing ongoing Revival for not just one or two months. No, as a matter of fact, their Churches have been in "Continuous Revival" from six to twenty years!

Just to hear the questions asked them by Michael and their responses is worth the price of the book alone. So much knowledge and wisdom are gleaned from their answers! These are men of God whom the Lord has raised up to spearhead a Last Day Apostolic

Move of God!

This book, the Wow Factor, is a Gift from God to the Pastor and Layperson alike who is Hungry for Revival! Not a Revival that starts on Sunday and ends on Wednesday, but a Revival that transforms them and their Church to be a Habitation of the Most High God!

This is a must have book that should be in every Pastor's Library; not in the section that gathers dust but the one that sits on your desk that you can go back to again and again and use as a reference tool. It is an Acts Two Outpouring Dictionary!

I have had the privilege and blessing of knowing Michael and Linda Livengood for approximately 30 years, and I have over the course of these years seen such spiritual growth in both Michael and Linda. But what I have marveled at the most is the revelation of truth, knowledge, and wisdom that has been imparted to them by the Holy Spirit. Their quest to know God and to see Revival in the Body of Christ is a result of how they pursue His Presence in the Prayer room and in their study of His Word.

Together they have written many books and study guides, but this book written by Michael, "The Wow Factor", is by far his greatest accomplishment. It is more than just a book. It is a Holy Ghost manuscript that prepares the Body of Christ (His Church) to be the recipients of a Holy Ghost Revival that is to be a Perpetual Revival till Christ comes to take his children home."

--*Prophet Fred Aguilar*

"This book comes from the author's heart. Here we find not so much an academic, historical, or theological discussion of "Revival – Awakening – Outpouring." We *do* find a heart-to-heart testimony of Michael and Linda Livengood's personal experience over recent decades. As an international evangelist and revivalist, the hungering pursuit of God is the Life-giving fountain from which this book flows. I sensed this vibrant passion when hearing and meeting Michael during a fruitful local Tent Mission February 2016.

I am grateful for this straight-forward, strong account. Michael writes from a different "stream of grace" than this reviewer. A new appreciation of his ethos is available here to understand and learn from. Although important, such fresh *information* is a stepping stone to inspiration and impartation; as the Spirit's eagerly desired *visitation* is to His longed-for *habitation* – "with us to *dwell."* In the "Outpourings" detailed here, prominence given to divine bodily healing and to the exercise of *charismata*, are main *differences* from the Awakenings with which I am more familiar. Yet the spiritual fruitfulness for the Kingdom is remarkably *similar,* see pages 5 – 7 onwards.

Particularly helpful is a stress on God's sovereignty in sending forth the full tide of the Spirit's outpouring; balanced with our human responsibility to expectantly prepare by "hungering and thirsting" for Him in overflowing Presence. These complementary Scriptural truths shine through succeeding chapters. Michael's wide experience amply illustrates the delights, difficulties, and dangers of "An Outpouring." Sections of "garnered wisdom" also offer practical help to revival leaders and followers – all who humbly, sacrificially, joyfully, *supremely*, desire the Grace and Glory of God to burst upon (*Wow!),* dwell in, and bring Heaven to earth in our congregations and communities. WITH ALL GLORY TO THE REVIVING LORD!"

--Roy N. McKenzie D. Min., Presbyterian minister, Gore, Southland, New Zealand. Co-author of Evangelical Revivals in New Zealand, (A survey history, with some basic principles of revival), 1999, 2016; and Choose the Lord, Here and Now! (19th century evangelism in New Zealand), 2016.

the
WOW
FACTOR

Michael Livengood

W2W

publishing

ISBN-13: 978-1981967919
ISBN-10: 1981967915
For Worldwide Distribution
Printed in the U.S.A.

Word 2 Word Publishing
Sikeston, MO
email: word2wordministries@gmail.com

FOREWORD

I have known Michael and Linda Livengood for more than twenty years. They were in hot pursuit of God before I met them at the Brownsville Revival and have avidly continued that pursuit around the world since I first met them.

This book is the result of their unrelenting desire to know God and the quest of the revival in which He wants His church to live.

Whether shooting the white-water rapids of the river of revival or reflecting in the calmer pools which occur after the rapids, Michael gives essentials necessary for understanding a God sent revival. He not only provides the insight of a gifted evangelist but includes perspectives from gifted pastors, apostles, prophets, and teachers who have taken the plunge in the river of revival with him.

I almost wrote, "If you have no desire for or fear revival, there is no need to read further." However, I had a check in my spirit. Even if you are fearful or lack desire, I urge you to read on. I write that because I believe every genuine born-again believer has an insatiable desire to know God in a greater way.

A careful, prayerful digest of the contents of this book will prompt hunger for and reassurance about a genuine move of God.

Go for it! And be blessed far beyond anything you have been blessed with thus far!

--Carey Robertson, former Senior Associate Pastor the Brownsville Revival, Brownsville Assembly of God, Pensacola, Florida

CONTENTS

1

WHAT DOES REVIVAL LOOK LIKE?

"Oh, that thou wouldest rend the heavens, that thou wouldest come down." – Isa 64:1

How many prayer meetings have you attended where you heard someone cry out to God for revival? Posts on Facebook will often express the desire for revival. Indeed, there are numerous groups on Facebook who exist for the purpose of calling people to revival.

But what does revival look like? How will you know when your church is in revival? The great Brownsville revival of the last century is often thought of as having started on Father's Day of 1995. Yet some in the church told me they felt like they were in revival before that famous day. I am not making this observation to create controversy, but rather to draw attention to three things. First, it can be hard to define when a revival begins. If there is a suddenly moment, such as Father's Day of 1995 in Pensacola, then it is easy to call that the beginning of revival. I would not argue with those who point to that event as the beginning. Certainly, that was when God took that which was hidden and brought it into the light. Second, it is to be aware that revival is often more of a journey than an event. Third, it is to be aware that people, churches, and cities are at different places on that journey. So, I do not want to be so legalistic as to fail to recognize a heaven-sent revival, simply because it does not tick all my boxes. At the same time, I am satisfied that some things have been called revival when they probably did not deserve such a title. Attempting to define revival leaves me a bit overwhelmed. Definitions of it abound, and minds much greater than mine have given us some excellent definitions. Perhaps my favorite choice is: "Revival is a community saturated with the Presence of God." Another definition I like is "God was tired of being misrepresented and decided to turn up and represent Himself."

In the year 2000, I was invited to preach four days at a church in one of the suburbs of Wellington, the capital of New Zealand. Those four days ultimately became 20 weeks of nightly services.

During those meetings, which were a part of the history of a local church revival that had been going on since the mid-1990s, the pastor of a significant local mainline church asked for a meeting between his staff, the staff at the church where I was preaching and me.

I was under the impression his church was the fourth or fifth largest church of its denomination in New Zealand, so when the meeting was arranged, I was a bit nervous. I had already gone through a meeting with two pastors and spouses of my denomination who had reservations over the meetings. I also knew a large number of people from his church had been attending the revival services, and I assumed the pastor was probably somewhat unhappy with me over this.

After the traditional cup of tea and getting settled into our seats, the pastor began to explain why he had asked for the meeting. He told us he was aware of at least fifty of his people who had attended the meetings, including most of his staff. I began to feel better when he observed, "The fruit of the meetings has been good." He went on to make four observations about those who had been attending the revival services.

These four things alone may not be revival, but I believe pastors will be satisfied with them until revival breaks out. So, let me share the four things he observed and then add one more to them, suggesting that when revival comes to your church, it may indeed look like the following.

First, this pastor observed, "Those who have been attending the revival have quit sinning." Second, he said, "Those who have been attending the revival have fallen in love with Jesus." His third observation was, "I cannot get the people who are attending the revival services to go home after church." And his final statement was, "Those who are attending your revival services are now asking me, 'Pastor, what can I do to help you'?"

As I listened to his description of what was taking place in his church, I realized he was describing a pattern I had been watching in many churches. Purity of life … fresh love for Jesus … a fresh love for God's House … and a desire to work for Jesus had been trademarks of every genuine revival I had been a part of. I realized the only thing he had missed was a testimony about numbers of people coming into the Kingdom of God. Later I discovered that since the meetings had broken open in his city that he had begun giving salvation altar calls in his church and people were coming to Jesus!

Rather than giving a scholarly definition of revival, let me suggest that when revival comes to your church, these five things are indeed likely to happen. Let us look at them now in more detail.

An Unusually Large Number of People Getting Saved!

At some point, genuine revival will cause people to be added to the Kingdom of God. Revival will lead to people getting saved! I use the expression "an unusually large number of people" very intentionally. An unusually large number varies depending on the situation. For example, if a church averages 3,000 in attendance per weekend and 15 people get saved one weekend that may not necessarily be revival. That might not be an unusually large number of people. However, if a church averages thirty people in attendance every weekend and five people get saved, I would suggest that might be considered an unusually large number of people. When a church is in revival, they will probably see unusually large numbers of people getting saved regularly.

This is not to say people getting saved is the only measure of a revival. Evangelism can occur outside the context of revival, but revival rarely occurs without evangelism happening. As an evangelist, I have been involved in many different types of evangelistic events. For example, I participated for some years in an event called Chicago Outreach which was sponsored by the youth department of my denomination. It was a great event. Some years more than 1,000 people would make commitments to Jesus. The Outreach involved street evangelism and open-air services in the parks of inner city Chicago. I passed out tracts. I invited people to the event planned for the park. I prayer-walked neighborhoods. I preached on the steps of churches. It was a great season in my life, but I would not have called it revival. It was evangelism. However, when revival breaks out evangelism becomes easier.

It is reported that during the Hebrides Revival of the 1950s in Scotland a man came to one of the pastors and told him he wanted to get saved. When the pastor indicated he had not seen the man at any of the meetings, the man responded by saying, "I have not been to the meetings, but this revival is in the air, and I cannot escape it. I must give my life to Jesus." The "open heavens" of a revival makes it easier for people to get saved.

A number of years ago an international ministry came to New Zealand to hold evangelistic events across the nation. Power teams, music teams, gymnastics, and many other creative evangelistic efforts took place. The events were surrounded by intercessory prayer. As an evangelist, I loved what was taking place. However, to be candid, the longed-for national revival did not occur. When people asked me at the time if this outreach would trigger revival in the nation, I indicated I hoped so, but I suspected it was the wrong horse. Evangelism alone does not bring revival, but I repeat, when revival comes evangelism will become more effective.

On the other hand, I can point to a planned day of ministry at a church in New Zealand that turned into a significant church revival. The one day became nineteen weekends (Friday nights through Sunday nights) or nearly 75 services. Over 225 people responded to a salvation altar call in a church that had been averaging roughly 180 on a Sunday morning. During those weekends attendance at the church peaked at nearly 340. During that time, the church had also been hosting a school for evangelism. Some of the evangelists at that school wanted me to go with them to the local elementary school so they could show me "real evangelism." I did accompany them, and to their apparent great surprise did everything they did just as well or better! I finally explained to them that I had been doing this type of evangelism for years. And I loved watching what God did in these events. However, experience had taught me that if revival broke open in a church … or a city … or a region, evangelism simply became more effective. As an evangelist, I love revival because it should lead to an increase in the number of souls getting saved.

During the days of the great Brownsville Revival, the open heavens affected the whole region. We visited that revival many times, and I discovered it was not difficult to strike up conversations with people about the Lord. The lady at a checkout counter talked about getting saved at the revival. A man at an ice cream shop asked me if I was in town to attend the revival and volunteered the information that he now attended every week. Conversation about Jesus seemed to be on the lips of people throughout the city. In fact, the very first time I visited the revival I asked the hosts at the campground if they could point me to the Brownsville Assembly of God. Immediately, from nearly 30 miles, they pinpointed the exact location of the church. That may not seem like a big deal to you, but as one who traveled in the days before GPS, it was a big deal. Very few people would immediately know the location of the local Assemblies of God church. I have even asked for directions to a particular church at a gas station only to be told they had never heard of it. Then I discovered the church was located directly behind the petrol station and they shared a common dumpster for rubbish!

When revival comes, the spiritual nursery of the church will become full of new spiritual babies!

Purity of Life

The mainline church pastor indicated those who had been attending the revival across town had quit sinning. Genuine revival produces change within the lives of believers!

During that nineteen-week meeting mentioned above, pastoral staff said to me, "We have never seen our people at this level of purity." Encounters with the manifest Presence of God at the altar were producing changes within the lives of the people. I draw just three stories out of many in that move.

One man who had been struggling with alcoholism awoke one morning during the meeting to see the early morning light form a cross that fell over the bottle of alcohol sitting next to his bed. Conviction settled on him. When the pastoral staff arrived at the office, he was sitting in the car park (parking lot) waiting for them. The flow of revival changed his life. I am aware any skeptic would have a field day with the coincidence of a cross covering the bottle of beer. However, for this man in the atmosphere of an open heaven, it was a clear word from God for him. These types of coincidences seem to occur regularly in revival.

Another man testified of the change in his family. His kids had gotten saved. He also reported his family had told him, "You have changed." His marriage had been on the brink of failure, and the revival restored it.

What Does Revival Look Like?

One mother reported her son had told her, "Mum, I love this revival. It has made you much nicer."

I love the stuff of revival. I love manifestations such as people being overcome by the Spirit of God and as a result not being able to stand. I love the necessity of a wheelchair being required to transport some from the meetings because they were so overcome by the Spirit of God they could not walk without help. I love the signs and wonders. We will come back to these subjects. However, my favorite stories of revival are of radically changed lives.

During another revival, my wife and I were at a salon getting haircuts. The beautician began to tell me how the revival had completely changed her family. This church was large enough that I did not recognize all attendees. I finally asked her to identify her family. When she gave me the name, I immediately recognized it. Just a few nights before her father had stood at the altar with tears flowing down his face as he tried to describe to me what was happening in his life. He said, "I can never go back to what life was like before." Today he is a pastor of an Assemblies of God church. The fruit of revival is the transformed life. As I write this chapter, he and his congregation are hosting what has become a multiple week outpouring of God's Spirit at their church.

I sat with the wife of a pastor where we had held a multi-week meeting as we discussed an upcoming funeral. A dear, elderly man had gone to be with the Lord. I was sharing how this sweetheart of a man would send me the most encouraging little emails with a phrase from Scripture tucked inside. She looked at me and said, "You still do not get it, do you? You still do not realize the depth of what God did during those twenty weeks." When I expressed my confusion at her remarks, she went on to tell me that prior to the revival that old man had been mean and cantankerous. She finally gave me the name of another gentleman whose life did not reflect much sweetness and said the man who had died was just like this person. I was stunned. Revival had produced an amazing change in him.

The Wow Factor

That same meeting produced one of the greatest stories I tell. I walked into the office one morning to be told by the office staff that the previous night had produced the greatest miracle they had seen. My mind began to spin back to the events of the previous night, but I honestly could not think of anything that would measure up to that level. I wandered down the hallway to the pastor's office. He invited me in with the news that I would always have an open pulpit at that church because last night he had seen the greatest miracle of his life. I finally said to him, "Pastor it is obvious to me that everyone but me knows what happened last night, so please tell me what happened?"

He went on to describe a gray-haired lady who had responded to the invitation the night before. She had been lying on the floor so quiet for so long we honestly thought she might have died. At one point the pastor had gotten down and placed his ear next to her mouth to see if she was still breathing! He could then hear her very, very softly asking Jesus to forgive her. It turned out this lady had once served in a school where her methods of discipline were rather extreme. She was considered one of the meanest persons in the city where she lived. There was a long list of injured people in her life.

She had already been to the church office earlier that morning. She sought to make restitution, to discover what she could do to make right the wrongs of her life. By the grace of God forgiveness had come into her life and one fruit of that repentance was the willingness to make right what was wrong. That fruit has lasted in her life.

When revival comes, people began to look like Jesus. Sin no longer has dominion over them.

Fresh Love for Jesus!

That mainline pastor observed that those impacted by revival fell in love with Jesus all over again. That sounds so simple. It sounds so obvious. I mean all Christians love Jesus, right? Well, yes

… and no.

Sometimes the stuff of church life can get in the way of our simple love relationship with Jesus. Professionalism can creep into the life of the preacher. We learn the techniques and the expectations. We know how to perform, and we learn what performances are required of us. The parishioner can get caught up in the routines as well. Church can become little different than a service club. Religion can eat away at relationship.

Revelation 2:4 describes this danger. The Holy Spirit rebuked the church at Ephesus because *"You have left your first love."* (NKJV) This usually does not happen overnight, nor is it intentional. Slowly we get caught up with stuff. Hurts happen in the church. Temptation comes. Schedules take control in our lives, and time with Jesus begins to be squeezed out. Religious activity continues, but the life of the relationship is gone.

During revival, our first love is renewed again. My wife describes her personal experience at the famous Brownsville revival with the following, "I felt like I got saved all over again." First love was being renewed. My personal experience was similar. Prayer was alive again. It was not just a daily discipline. Now it was a joy. I looked forward to my time with Jesus more than any other event of the day. I would almost scheme to pray. I would wake up singing. It did not matter how late I had gone to bed the night before. The song I had lost had been restored. Jesus was first place again.

This theme of falling in love with Jesus all over again is clearly a part of the testimonies of revival.

Fresh Love for God's House

This pastor next said to us, "I cannot get those who have been attending the revival services to go home."

It may sound humorous, but there is truth in his statement. Most pastors do not deal with this problem. Most pastors have two other problems. First, how do I get the people to come to church?

The second is how do I get them to be present when they are there?

During revival, church attendance becomes less duty and more delight. Instead of groaning at the prospect of going to church again, people begin to measure time by how long it will be before they get to go to church again.

One father explained to me that he and his wife had a new dilemma. Before the revival broke out in their church, they would have disagreements over which one had to go to church and which one had the privilege of staying home with the children. Now, he said they disagreed over who got to go to church and who had to stay home with the children. It seemed to me the solution was to bring the children with them to church! However, the point of this story was revival had changed their mindset about attending church.

As one young lady said to a friend, who had invited her to church, "I love your church, you have fun." In times of revival church becomes fun, so the people love to be there.

During a twenty-week revival in New Zealand, we finally had to insist people leave the building at midnight so that the auditorium could be cleaned and prepared for the next day. The atmosphere of revival is such that people do not want to leave. They will often simply linger around the altar or sit in their seats and soak up the presence of God.

Related to this is a time phenomenon. During significant revival, time seems irrelevant. I tell more of our personal Brownsville revival story in chapter one of my book "The Glory Factor," but I want to share part of my story here. The Sunday morning service at Brownsville Revival in Pensacola, Florida began at 10 am. I was shocked when hunger pangs caused me to check my watch for the first time, and I discovered it was nearly 2 pm. I had been in church for four hours! I do not believe church has to last forever for it to be "God." I have seen a lot of fluff in church. I have been in services where it took nearly 30 minutes to make the announcements or notices. Long services do not necessarily mean God is in it. On the other hand, when revival breaks out in a church, services often become longer. People love hanging out in God's Presence. Worship is no longer perfunctory. Expectation goes through the roof. People will sit on the edge of their seat to hear the Word of God preached. In fact, some will feel deprived if the service is too short! Church is not endured … it is enjoyed!

We relate to the words of David in Psalm 122:1, *"When they said, 'Let's go to the house of GOD,' my heart leaped for joy."* (Message Translation)

Yes, revival makes church fun again!

A Desire to Work for Jesus

The final thing this pastor observed was the rise in volunteers. Those who were attending the revival were coming and asking, "How can we help you, Pastor?"

Such a response from the people could create a heart attack!

A revived person looks for an opportunity to give away what God has done in them. This does not come from condemnation nor manipulation. It comes from overflow.

During one fifteen-week revival meeting, a man in the church began showing up during the day on his own accord to clean the auditorium and prepare it for the night's service. So, each day found him cleaning the tissue papers from around the altar and placing the songbooks back in the racks on the pews. In the same meeting, another businessman would come early every night to make follow up telephone calls to those who had gotten saved the night before. Nobody had recruited him. He simply wanted to find a tangible way to release what God was doing inside of him.

One pastor described to me how revival had changed every department in his church. First and foremost was the sense of Presence and purpose that had come. But it had not stopped there. When revival is taking place working in the Kingdom is a joy and a priority. The pool of volunteers normally increases in revival. This does not mean every potential ministry will have volunteers standing in line. Indeed, some church ministries may cease during revival. It does suggest that people tend to want to work for Jesus when He has done a work inside of them.

Revival is a part of the answer to the prayer of Jesus in Luke 10:2, *"The harvest is plentiful, but the workers are few. Ask the Lord of the harvest, therefore, to send out workers into his harvest field."* (NIV)

Revival raises up workers!

Yes, But…

I can hear someone say yes, but all the above should be a part of every church. It should be a part of normal church life.

Absolutely!

This is why many have observed that revival is God taking that which was abnormal and returning it to normal.

Another student of revival observed revival is God compressing into a short period that which normally takes longer. It is not God doing what never has happened. It is God restoring and enhancing what we should expect to be church life.

It is the pastor who said to me during a fifteen-week meeting in his church, "Do you realize that we now are seeing the type of conversions normally seen in the average church once a generation once a week?"

The above descriptions of what happens in revival are not intended to limit what God does to only those things. Indeed, in the following chapter, we will explore some other aspects of revival. It is to suggest that these are good starting points for revival. These should be things all of us can agree we want to see in our churches. More people to be saved … to be sanctified … to be lovers of Jesus … to be lovers of His house … to be workers in His vineyard.

2

FIVE STAGES OF REVIVAL

*"The Lord, whom ye seek, shall suddenly
come to his temple." – Mal 3:1*

Because revival is more of a journey than an event, it will have stages. However, these stages are not always clearly distinguished. One stage does not end for the next one to begin. Rather they build on one another or blend from one into the next. Each stage does not replace the previous phase. Because revival can be both corporate and personal a congregation may appear to be going through one stage corporately while individuals are going through another stage personally. Indeed, once revival breaks out and becomes a part of church life, all five stages may occur simultaneously.

Stage One: Wow!

I call the first stage of revival WOW! Many historical revivals had what is defined as a "suddenly" moment. The concept of the suddenly is based on Malachi 3:1(NAS95), *"And the Lord, whom you seek, will suddenly come to His temple."* It is that moment when the God who is omnipresent chooses to reveal Himself. The revelation may come as an act or a miracle, but typically this first WOW is more all-consuming than that.

This moment is less about what He does and more about who He is! The atmosphere suddenly fills with Him. When I think of this WOW I am reminded of the Welsh lady my pastor father was fond of talking about who would say concerning Jesus, "It is better felt than telt." This WOW of revival sometimes leads to terrible theological statements where people say things like, "He is here." Of course; we know He has always been here. He is omnipresent. Or we say things like, "God came." How does One who is omnipresent "go" somewhere? However, we are left without a better description of the event. I suppose technically I could say, "I became aware He was there," but for most people, the former statements better describe what we are experiencing. We are blown away with Him. The greatest services for me are often the hardest to write about because they are not jammed full of statistics. Sometimes those services have been moments when the Presence of God was so thick it felt hard to breathe. I did not want to move lest I offend either the Holy Spirit or distract some in the service. There are several services that I call "My top five services." I am hard pressed to pick one above the other.

One occurred in 1996 in Michigan City, Indiana. My family and I had been invited to participate in a weekend of reconciliation between two churches. I was scheduled to speak on the Saturday night and Sunday services. After preaching my sermon and praying with the fifteen or twenty who had responded to the salvation altar call, I felt I was to pray for the two lead pastors of the churches involved in the reconciliation weekend. As I did, both they and their wives were overcome by the presence and power of God and collapsed on the floor. I felt impressed to then pray for the members of the pastoral staffs, deacons, elders, and their spouses. I planned to "lay hands" on these twenty-four people. However, we never got that far. I was still on the platform and twenty feet away from the line of people that had formed at the altar when I felt what I could only describe as a power surge that went past me. Without me touching a single person twenty-four people collapsed on the floor much like dominos. The gasp from the 200 plus in the auditorium was audible. I turned to my wife and son to ask if they had experienced what I had just felt. The answer was a definite "Yes." The Presence that invaded that altar service pretty much stayed, not only for the next fifteen weeks of nightly services but for most of the next year.

Perhaps two years after that we were in a meeting at a church in Indianapolis. The schedule was for four days, but the meetings ran for seven weeks (Wednesday through Sunday). From the first day, it was obvious God was up to something, but the highlight for me was Sunday night of week five. During the first week of the meeting, the pastor felt the Lord gave him a word about something that would happen after the fourth week, so he asked us to clear our schedule and just keep doing the meetings. On week five he asked me to preach the Sunday morning service since he had preached the preceding two himself. The message God gave me was very confrontational. Conviction fell in that auditorium! I did not lay hands on anyone, but most of the congregation were on their faces crying out to God. When we stepped back into the Sunday night meeting, we experienced the WOW. The Presence of God was evident from before the first song. Wave after wave of God crashed upon that place. The pastor told me he was afraid to touch the keyboard because God was in the room, and I told the youth pastor I was not going anywhere near the pulpit for the same reason. For many years afterward, I only needed to identify that service by saying it was "the Sunday night at *****" and anyone who had been in that meeting would nod their heads in agreement. Every sinner got saved, but it was not my sermon. There was a Presence beyond my ability to describe. On the following Tuesday night prayer meeting, I asked the 75 or so assembled there if they had tried to explain Sunday night to anyone. Everyone in that room had attempted to do so. I then asked how many found they could not adequately describe the night. Once again, the verdict was unanimous. Nobody felt they could give an adequate description of that service. Our vocabularies were not sufficient.

A twenty-week revival in New Zealand had many WOW moments, but one is uppermost in my thinking. It happened on a Sunday morning in a pre-service prayer time. The pastor and I were already looking at extending the meetings because of what we sensed, but in that pre-service prayer time, it was like the Lord put His approval on what we were thinking. While we were praying, it was like the entire room was hit by the Presence of God with most of the 40 or so prayer warriors ending up on the floor. We had to drag the worship team to their feet to send them to the auditorium to lead worship. I joined them 20 minutes later. We were 45 minutes into the service before the last of the stragglers made their way into the auditorium. The pastor was in that last group. However, since he still could not walk he was brought in by a wheelchair. The pre-planned service order never occurred. No offering was received. My sermon changed. However, when I gave an invitation to get right with God, there was no space left at the altar. Then another spiritual explosion followed. It was 2 pm before everything wound down. The Lord's entrance also signaled the launch of the twenty weeks.

Our hearts cry out for Him to come so we can say, "WOW!"

Stage Two: Wow!

The second stage of a revival is WOW! That's right, the same word. However, where the first WOW focuses on who He is, the overwhelming sense that God Himself has chosen to "walk into the room" producing the indefinable sense of Him, this stage focuses on what He does.

This second stage is the release of miracles, healing, signs, wonders, manifestations, and so forth. We believe these kinds of things should be part and parcel of normal Christianity. However, while many churches and ministries do have healing ministries, the existence of these things alone does not indicate that revival has come. On the other hand, when revival does come, these things will often either increase or occur more easily. Some historians may observe that many revivals have not been marked by the miraculous, and this is true. However, other revivals have clearly been marked by miracles and supernatural phenomena.

I submit that the revival described in the New Testament was certainly one accompanied by signs and wonders. There are 39 references to signs and wonders of some sort in 33 different passages in the book of Acts. Appendix one gives a breakdown of both those passages and the signs and wonders they describe.

In the book, "Azusa Street - They Told Me Their Stories," which is a compilation of testimonies from the Azusa street revival, miracles, signs, and wonders play a prominent part. On pages 37-38 the writer noted that "although the Shekinah Glory was present all the time within the building, this divine connection wasn't an everyday occurrence. Whenever this connection was present, the power of God was even more intense within the meeting." On page 99 another participant in the Azusa revival said, "The greater the Shekinah Glory, the greater the power." [1]

James Burns wrote a book in 1909 entitled "Revivals, Their Laws, and Leaders." A portion of that book was re-published by World Wide Publications in 1993 under the title, "The Laws of Revival." In that book, Burns discusses not only the conditions preceding and leading up to revival but also the things that happen during revival. He observed the four things that precede revival are: sin, suffering, supplication, and salvation. When revival comes, he noted these four things occur: sin is exposed (great conviction falls on people with many conversions), much prayer continues,

---

[1] Azusa Street: They Told Me Their Stories. Copyright @ 2006 by Tom Welchel. Published by Dare2Dream Books, Mustang, Oklahoma. (kindle version) p 37-38

phenomena (supernatural events) are seen, there are opposition and persecution. All of these deserve additional attention, but for this chapter, I draw your attention to what Burns' called phenomena alone. These are the signs and wonders. In some revivals, they have come in the form of healing and other miracles. In other revivals events such as trances, falling under the power of God and gifts of the Holy Spirit are prominent. These are what I call the "stuff" of revival. I love these events, but also recognize these phenomena often become controversial leading to opposition and persecution. Manifestations such as falling to the floor, shaking, trances, being "drunk" in the Spirit often occur during this stage. It is people being overwhelmed by Him. It is God not only announcing Himself by His entrance but also demonstrating what He would like to do.

In my personal experience, the greatest revivals I have been a part of began with the WOW of His presence followed by the WOW of His power. It seems the stronger the Presence, the easier it becomes for people to receive the power of God.

The outpouring that began in August of 2010 in Terre Haute, Indiana, and continues at the time of this writing has seen thousands of people both saved and healed. Interestingly, I preached on healing only once or twice in the first two years of that move. Yet the stronger the manifest Presence of God becomes the easier healing comes. Many of those healings have come as a direct result of the revelatory gifts of the Spirit, but others have simply come during seasons of worship.

Bring again the WOW of what You do, Lord!

Stage Three: Ouch!

Stage three is often the most challenging phase for people. I call it the OUCH stage. This is the fire turned inward. This is where the Spirit of God turns His focus on the personal life of the individual in the revival. The fire is to purge. John the Baptist references this aspect of revival in Luke 3:16-17, *"John answered them all, 'I baptize you with water. But one more powerful than I will come, the thongs of whose sandals I am not worthy to untie. He will baptize you with the Holy Spirit and with fire. His winnowing fork is in his hand to clear his threshing-floor and to gather the wheat into his barn, but he will burn up the chaff with unquenchable fire.'* These two verses suggest the stages I am writing about. He will baptize with the Holy Spirit. This is renewal. This is a different expression than WOW, but it is essentially the same thing.

Not only will He baptize with the Holy Spirit, but this baptism will also be with "fire," and He will "clear his threshing floor." The KJV uses the expression "thoroughly purge." Purity is the intent of this action of the Spirit. It is the OUCH.

As a revival deepens, it begins to change the lives of those it touches. My wife and I have observed certain patterns that exist in those God moments that turn into extended meetings. Often the first couple of weeks of those kinds of meetings are full of the WOW moments. Testimonies reflect that. However, somewhere around week three, a subtle change begins to occur among those who have been a part of every meeting. The longer they spend in the Presence of God the more that fire begins to purify them. Sin is exposed. Not just the big sins. Often this is not the outward sin that we think of. Rather this involves changes in attitudes. Small sins become unbearable. The desire to be pure before Him becomes stronger and stronger. I call it OUCH because sometimes it is not pleasant. We begin to see things about ourselves we had not noticed before. The brighter the light of His Presence the more we see in ourselves that is not as it should be. Have you ever attempted to clean up a room that is not well lit? As well as you think you have done, you are often amazed when the light is turned on, and you see things you had not noticed before. The purifying fire both reveals and then purges us.

It is at this stage that some mistakenly believe revival is over. They do not realize God places as much value on the OUCH as He does on the WOW. Now, I admit I love the WOW. I love the Presence of God that is so thick I am either hesitant to move, or unable to do so. I also love the WOW of the deeds of God. I love the testimonies of those who have been healed. I love needing wheelchairs to carry people out of meetings. I love the nights we need designated drivers because others are simply too drunk in the Spirit to be allowed behind a steering wheel. But the OUCH stage is critical to what God is doing. The theological term for it is sanctification.

Those who are willing to embrace this stage will be able to enter the last two stages. Those who run from this stage will never realize the fulfillment of God's purposes for them in revival. Those who desire to become carriers of the Presence of God do embrace this stage and allow the fire of revival to burn the chaff out of them. This stage cannot be short-circuited. It must be walked through.

Are we ready to say, "Ouch?"

Stage Four: Oohh…

This stage unveils the purpose of God in revival. Luke 3:17 describes this stage in the words, *"Gather the wheat into his garner."* The heart of God is always turning toward *"lost sheep."* The great commission has to do with preaching the gospel to the lost. The previous three stages motivate and equip us toward this commission.

As revival moves along, we begin to catch more and more of God's heart. We begin to feel what He feels toward those who do not know Him. Meals at a cafe become opportunities to share with or pray with a waitress or waiter. The open heavens atmosphere makes conversations about Jesus more natural.

During one revival service, siblings on opposite ends of the altar began crying out to God for the salvation of another sibling. Neither was aware of the prayer of the other, but both had been moved on by Holy Spirit compassion for their unsaved brother. Later that night the pastor, his wife, my wife and I decided to have something to eat and enjoy a little fellowship. We were unaware these siblings were crying out to God for the salvation of their brother, but we "chanced" to go to the same restaurant where he worked. While we were sitting at the table, he came out of the kitchen to our table and asked the pastor if he was the pastor of ***** church and indicated he needed to talk to him. At 2 am in the parking lot of that restaurant, he surrendered his life to Jesus. Approximately four hours had passed since his siblings had been at the throne of grace calling out his name. Revival had stirred their hearts for the lost.

The pastor of a fifteen-week revival told me one of the spinoffs from the revival had been the increased burden for the lost that had developed in his church. Night after night people had given their hearts to Jesus, leading to an increased awareness of the lost. People had a new burden and passion for their unsaved friends and relatives. He told me he would do the whole thing over, even if none of the nearly 500 people who had gotten saved had done so, just because of the burden for the lost that had come into his church.

The Great Commission was always in the congregation's Bibles, but there was something about the atmosphere of revival that made it a living passion for them. They had caught the OOHH…!

Indeed, revivals that never reach the OOHH… stage rarely last long. During the revival of the 90s, a pastor of one of the well-known revival churches of my denomination put out a letter that came into my hands. He acknowledged the revival had lost momentum because they had lost the OOHH… They had turned inward what God wanted to be turned outward.

Some may say "But we don't need revival to witness," and I would not disagree. However, something about the WOW inspires us to the OOHH… Let me make two very important observations at this point.

First, churches that attempt to accomplish the OOHH… without the WOW tend to burn out their members. Condemnation sets in. People struggle in the energy of their flesh to work for Jesus because we know we should. Some succeed, but many simply grow weary in the well-doing. Our churches are full of people who have been burned out in church work. It is the WOW that motivates us. It is the WOW moments that release anointing to accomplish the assignment of the OOHH… Remember, Jesus did not give the disciples the final release into ministry until after He sent them to the upper room. Pentecost was a WOW moment that empowered the church to fulfill the OOHH…

My second observation is this. Those revival churches that forget the OOHH… do not sustain the revival. Heavens will not remain open if we forget why God opened them. During the revival season of the late 1990s, I was the preacher of a revival in a midwestern state where the entire cheerleading squad of the local school got saved. The tangible presence of God was awesome. One night it seemed "the river" was thigh high. One elderly saint described it to me as "old-time Pentecost." God had come again. Roughly a year later, I was preaching at the same church, except that the atmosphere was much different. The pastor reminded me that at the close of the first meetings I had asked the church what they were going to do with what God had done in their midst? He said the answer became inward focused. They wanted "to sing, shout, dance about and fall on the floor." Now, I love to do all four of those things. However, they were not interested in the OOHH… They wanted to keep things contained inside the four walls of the building. As a result, the fire had quickly gone out.

I believe the WOW and the OUCH are to empower us for the OOHH…

Stage Five: Whoaaaah!

This is where God wants revival to go! This is where we no longer attend revival, but we have now become revival! Revival has become a part of our DNA. We breathe it …. sleep it …. eat it …. walk it. We begin to carry the Presence of God tangibly. When we walk into a room, the atmosphere changes. Praying with people in the marketplace becomes as common as praying in the church. Signs and wonders follow us as they followed Jesus.

WHOAAAH may not be a theological term, but those who have crossed into certain levels of revival relate to it. Life will never be the same. This is the group that has been ruined by revival. They have seen, at least in a small way, what revival is intended to produce, and they can never be happy with "normal" church life again.

My wife and I have been graced by God to be a part of many significant church revivals. Some have gone well beyond the walls of a local church. Some have impacted entire cities or entire regions. Yet, most of us who have been in such a move of God feel we have only scratched the surface of what God desires.

We relate to the promises of a "last days revival." Our hearts resonate with the Glory of the Lord covering the earth. I love to tell the stories of what Jesus does in revival, but I never tell the stories with the sense of having reached our destination. We believe there is more! We see the example of the New Testament church. We read the stories of the great revivals of history. We are aware of what He has done in our lives in revival, and we long to become revival in an even greater way. We know we have touched the borders of the possibilities. We long to enter into the fullness of WHOAAAH!

3

FIVE KEYS TO REVIVAL

"Blessed are they which do hunger and thirst after righteousness: for they shall be filled." - Mt 5:6

What attracts the Presence of God to some places while others never seem to experience that Presence? Why does an Outpouring occur in some cities and not in others?

From the outset of this chapter let me acknowledge two things. First, we must recognize the sovereignty of God. I sat with an Australian pastor whose church was experiencing sustained revival for a considerable amount of time. When I asked him for the why he began with the sovereignty of God. In fact, even after I share the keys of this chapter, the bottom line still comes down to a sovereign God. I think every church leader where I have ministered, and revival has come will point to the sovereignty of God. This is not to avoid our responsibility, but it does recognize there are aspects of a revival that go beyond our ability to analyze. It exceeds our pay grade.

Second, I do not have all the answers. Scripture says, *"We see through a glass darkly"* (1 Corinthians 13:12). However, I have sought to be a student of revival. Not only does my library contain many volumes on revival, not only have I attended some of the great revivals of our day, not only have I interviewed leaders of revival, not only have I been the lead evangelist at significant revivals, but I have constantly sought to understand the why. An apostolic friend of mine was asked why he did what he did. In response, he said "I don't know. I do it by instinct. Go ask Michael; he can explain why I do what I do." There is much I do not know, but there are some things I have learned, and these I now want to share with you.

Key Number One: Hunger

On the human side, I believe the primary prerequisite for the outpouring of revival is hunger. Most people will say the first requirement for revival is prayer. At the risk of sounding like a heretic, I would disagree. I would say the bottom line is hunger, which is usually expressed in prayer. I make this distinction for a couple of reasons. I want us to understand that revival is not so rote that a certain amount of prayer automatically guarantees a certain type of revival. God will not be placed in a box…even our good, religious box. Secondly, experience has challenged some of my earlier assumptions about revival.

When I look at the four longest revival meetings I have preached, interesting things become evident. All these revival meetings produced a revival bigger than the meetings I preached.

One of the four revivals occurred in a church that had a 50-year prayer meeting. When I say 50 years, I mean that church had a 24/7 prayer meeting for 50 years. During the dark days of World War II when Nazi Germany seemed invincible, in response to the plea of the King of England they began to pray and did not stop when the war ended. It was not hard to connect the dots on this one. That prayer meeting was clearly linked to what God did.

A second church had no prayer meeting at all! None! They had no official intercessors. During the meetings, the pastor would look at me and say, "Why is this happening? We do not even have a prayer meeting." During the run of the meeting, prayer gatherings were established, and personal intercessors for the pastor were born, but none were in place before the revival came.

A third church was experiencing spontaneous times of prayer. I believe they did have some structured prayer meetings, but the argument could be made the impact was coming out of these spontaneous prayer times. Text exchanges between several men and their pastor would lead to these times of prayer.

The fourth had neither intercessors nor an organized prayer meeting. In fact, the pastor had been burned in the past by intercessors, so he was cautious about having such a group in his church. He did have a few personal intercessors, but they were not a recognized group. There was a prayer ministry in his city, and he had been meeting with a group of local pastors weekly to pray for over ten years. He was certainly a pray-er.

However, all four had at least one thing common. They were hungry. Really hungry. I could go on to describe some of the things I saw and heard about these four pastors, but let me just say, "They were hungry."

Please do not misunderstand me. I am not putting prayer down. I am simply saying that behind the prayer was something even deeper. Matthew 5:6 promises a reward for those who are hungry. *"They shall be filled."* I would hasten to say again that hunger usually leads to prayer and prayer can deepen the hunger. I want to move beyond a rote understanding of this. The Brownsville Assembly of God had an awesome two-plus year Sunday night prayer meeting preceding that revival. It was clearly a part of the plan of God and the journey of revival. However other churches who started prayer meetings found two years was not a magic number. One pastor friend in Texas described a ten-year journey prior to the breaking out of a massive revival in his church.

If hunger is the first requirement, then what do we do to stir up the hunger?

Prayer is often a vital part of this.

Visiting revival centers has also often stirred hunger. Most of the above-mentioned pastors made trips to revival centers. They had personal encounters with God in those places. They saw what God could do. Some made repeated trips. It appears some of them received an anointing relating to revival while they were in those places.

Such travel may not be possible for all, so reading books on revival can stir hunger. That may be one of the reasons this book is in your hands. Watching videos or internet clips may also serve to do the same thing.

For most of the pastors mentioned above the hunger for revival was not a short-term event. They had been "going after God" for many years. Hunger had become a lifestyle.

God may lead you to start a revival prayer meeting. Go for it if He does so.

I don't think I have ever seen revival break out where hunger did not exist. Let the hunger drive you to the throne room. Desperate hunger seems to attract Him! Matthew 5:6 gives us this promise, *"Blessed are they which do hunger and thirst after righteousness: for they shall be filled."* The condition for the promise is a hunger and thirst after righteousness. This is more than for manifestations. This includes a hunger for righteousness, a hunger for being right with God. To be filled is to gorge or to supply in abundance. Those who are not hungry will not receive.

Isaiah chapter 55 extends an invitation to those who are hungry and thirsty. They can come to eat and drink that which God will supply for them. Tragically, some hungry people are looking in all the wrong places. They are spending their money, but it has not provided the food that is needed. This 55th chapter suggests two essentials are necessary in order to be filled. We must *"Seek the Lord while He may be found."* I must come on His terms. When God has released a river of His Spirit, we must come to that river. He will not send out a tributary for our convenience. We must come to that which He has supplied. God sets the terms for revival, and He will

28

not negotiate those terms. I not only must seek Him while He may be found, but I must quit sinning. In verse seven the call is for the wicked to *"forsake his way…and…return unto the Lord."* Mercy and pardon are promised to the one who will do this.

Minimally, hunger is seen in the following. First, it is seen in our desperation for God. Attendance at church or revival type of meetings usually happens. I challenge the genuineness of the hunger of the person who tells me he is desperate for revival but rarely shows up at church. Actions shout louder than words. Finally, this hunger will be seen in raw obedience to God. John 14: 21, *"He that hath my commandments, and keepeth them, he it is he that loveth me: and he that loveth me shall be loved of my Father, and I will love him and will manifest myself to him."* The manifestation of the Lord's presence is to the one who keeps His commandments.

Key Number Two: Holiness

In a previous chapter, I suggested one of the phases of revival is OUCH. I indicated that revival tends to expose sin in our lives and that sanctification or holiness tends to increase in revival. This holiness is cyclical. It seems that a certain level of it needs to be in place for Him to be attracted. I will perhaps oversimplify the thought with two maxims. To be sanctified is to be separated from sin and to be consecrated, or sold out to God. This thought of being sanctified (separated from sin and sold out to God) is essential in our journey to both heaven and participation in revival.

Our sanctification is commanded because of God's nature and our relationship to Him as His children. We are commanded in Leviticus 11:44, *"For I am the LORD your God: ye shall, therefore, sanctify yourselves, and ye shall be holy; for I am holy."* The command is given again in Leviticus 20:7, *"Sanctify yourselves, therefore, and be ye holy: for I am the LORD your God."*

John Wesley, the founder of Methodism, observes in his notes on Numbers 11:18, "Sanctifying is often used for preparing."

Revival rarely comes to the unprepared. In Numbers 11:18 the Israelites were to sanctify themselves in preparation for eating the quail God was about to send them. This sanctification should have included repentance for their grumbling and complaining against God's provision. In 1 Samuel 16:5 the elders of Bethlehem, along with Jesse and his sons, were commanded to sanctify themselves in preparation for a special time of sacrifice and feasting. Worship requires preparation of heart and life. Often, we want God to manifest His Presence in an awesome way in our services even though we have made little or no preparation for Him to show up. In 2 Chronicles 35:6 Josiah admonished the priests to sanctify themselves in preparation for the Passover and coming revival. Leadership must prepare itself to lead the people into a move of God. As spiritual priests, we are to sanctify ourselves for what God wants to do.

I believe that the key of holiness is of utmost importance. It is not the key of legalism - and I am not calling for legalistic actions. It is a call for consecration. I am calling you to make a complete cutting off of sin - to purpose not to tolerate any area of sin within your life. I am calling you to completely sell out to Him - to do His will. I believe it was John Knox who called for just a handful of men who feared God and nothing else. With those men, Knox believed he could change his nation.

We must sanctify ourselves to defeat the enemy. A call for sanctification is given in Joshua 7:13, *"Up, sanctify the people, and say, Sanctify yourselves against tomorrow: for thus saith the LORD God of Israel, There is an accursed thing in the midst of thee, O Israel: thou canst not stand before thine enemies, until ye take away the accursed thing from among you."* (KJV) The background to this passage is essential to understand what is happening. The people of God had earlier experienced an incredible victory when the city of Jericho fell to them. This opening round of the conquest of the promised land was over, but in the middle of that great victory, sin reared its head. Achan disobeyed God. Joshua 7:1 records his actions: *"Achan...took of the accursed thing"* and what he did had a major impact on the whole nation. *"The anger of the LORD was kindled against the children of Israel."* I am not looking to bring condemnation on anyone, but your actions impact others. Because of Achan's disobedience, the small town of Ai could not be taken. Even though the conquest of Ai was a part of the promise of God, it did not occur, and as a result, Joshua found himself on his face before God. Joshua 7:6 records it, *"And Joshua rent his clothes, and fell to the earth upon his face before the ark of the LORD until the eventide, he and the elders of Israel, and put dust upon their heads"* (KJV). He cries out his frustration and begins to question God. Why is this happening? Why were they unable to move into victory? Why did they come across Jordan? What about God's reputation?

Have you been there? "Lord, why are we not seeing what we want to see? Lord, why is the power of the enemy still so strong in my life … my church … my city … my nation? Lord, why wasn't I content to leave well enough alone? Why did we have to start pursuing revival? Why did I start reading this book?"

God's answer shocks Joshua. "Get up! Quit praying!" Usually, we expect to hear God say, "Pray more." However, God tells Joshua to quit praying. It was no longer time to petition Him. It was time to deal with the sin issue. The lessons of this incident must be learned. It was the will of God to take Ai. God wants you free from bondage. God wants you to experience revival. However, repentance from sin precedes deliverance. Israel would never see the city taken and the enemy defeated until sanctification took place.

By sinning the Israelites had removed themselves from a position of favor and blessing. Because they had *"taken of the accursed thing,"* (7:11) *"they were accursed."* (7:12). Jericho was called *"accursed"* in Joshua 6:17. Literally, that means it was a city devoted to destruction. Everything within the city was considered accursed, meaning that everything in the city had been given to God and was to be offered up as a sacrifice to Him. The "cursed" thing was either set aside as something holy unto the Lord or something

31

which was offensive to Him and needed to be destroyed. In Joshua 6:18 they had been warned to *"keep yourselves from the accursed thing, lest ye make yourselves accursed."* By taking hold of the accursed thing, they took upon themselves something of that accursed thing. The evangelist in me must express this warning. If you mess around with sin or things of the devil those things get a foothold in your life. Living in victory requires us to repent and renounce the accursed thing.

Until there is repentance and renunciation of sin, it seems your enemy, the devil, still has legal right to exercise influence or control over you in that area of your life. You must become sanctified, that is, set apart from the sin and then set apart to God. Perhaps these last few lines have been for you. You have struggled with being overcome by the devil. You have not yet let go of the sin...but today as you come to His altar in true repentance...as you repent, renounce, and turn away from whatever sin has snared you, you can walk into a victory you have never walked in before.

For the church to experience the revival we long to see, we must understand we cannot tolerate sin in our lives...we must deal with it ruthlessly. I am not saying the church should be ruthless toward those who have failed; I am saying I must purpose not to compromise with sin on a personal level. Some want to see strongholds coming down in cities, but this will not happen as long as there is sin in our lives. Until we deal with sin, Satan has legal permission to hang on to positions of power.

Secondly, we must sanctify ourselves to see signs and wonders. In Joshua 3:5 an impossible barrier was being faced by Israel. The Jordan River was flooded, and the nation needed to get across it to occupy their promised land. This certainly looked impossible in the normal order of things. As you read this, you may be facing impossible circumstances today, but the promise is *"tomorrow the LORD will do wonders among you."* Tomorrow the Lord will do a "God thing among you." God was about to do something for Joshua that only He could do, and it would bring glory only to Himself. By making a way through the flooded Jordan, He encouraged His people to believe that He was well able to bring them into the promised land.

Signs and wonders are specialties of heaven. God alone can do these great wonders. I believe signs and wonders both have a role to play in revival; they speak of a last day outpouring of the Lord's Spirit. We read in Acts 2:18-19, *"and on my servants and on my hand-maidens I will pour out in those days of my Spirit; and they shall prophesy: and I will show wonders in heaven above, and signs in the earth beneath; blood, and fire, and vapor of smoke"* (KJV). In Acts 2:22 Jesus was *"approved of God among you by miracles and wonders and signs."* Additionally Acts 2:43 says, *"many wonders and signs were done by the apostles."*

I submit to you that purity needs to precede power. We are looking for more of the power of God...when God wants us to be filled with His purity. Revival should include acts of God's power, but before this power was displayed in Joshua chapter 3, they were called to sanctify themselves. We need a cleansing work in our lives, so we can handle it when God sends His power.

Mike Bickle, the founder of the International House of Prayer, believes the Lord spoke to him about an end time revival that contains three elements. The first element would be wine, which speaks of refreshing and joy. The second element would be fire, which speaks of purity and holiness. And the final element would be wind, which speaks of signs and wonders. I am suggesting we will not truly encounter that third one (wind) until we deal with the question of sanctification.

Thirdly, we must sanctify ourselves to experience the manifest Presence of God. We must sanctify ourselves for the Presence of God to fully come. While many have experienced a measure of God's Presence, I submit the full potential of what God would like to do has not yet been reached. There is a difference between anointing and Presence, and I believe there may be a further step beyond this to Glory. The anointing is enduement of power for service. It is God working through you, but the anointing does not mean the human vessel is perfect.

The Presence, however, ministers to you. I have been in services where I felt the Presence of God, but little anointing or virtue flowed through me to others. I have also been in services where I felt very little of God's Presence, but His anointing flowed through me to others. I would suggest that when a strong level of Presence or a touch of Glory comes stuff happens. Consider what happened in Exodus 19 when God showed up. The Scripture describes thunders, lightning, thick cloud, the voice of the trumpet, fire, and the mountain shook.

If "revival seems to be when God is tired of man misrepresenting Him and shows up to represent Himself" as already noted in Chapter 1, then before God's Presence comes, sanctification must occur. It seems the more our flesh dies, the more of Him we can see. You can minister in the flesh, or you can crucify the flesh and see what God might do. Thus, Holiness or consecration is linked to the Presence of God.

We must sanctify ourselves to become carriers of God's Presence. Notice, 1Chronicles 15:12, *"And (David) said unto them, Ye are the chief of the fathers of the Levites: sanctify yourselves, both ye and your brethren, that ye may bring up the ark of the LORD God of Israel unto the place that I have prepared for it."* (KJV). In order to bring the ark into the place David had prepared for it the priests were instructed to sanctify themselves; only the priests were to carry the ark, and they had to be sanctified in order to do so.

We also notice 2 Chronicles 35:6, *"So kill the passover, and sanctify yourselves, and prepare your brethren, that they may do according to the word of the LORD by the hand of Moses"* (KJV). As a part of the great revival in the time of King Josiah, the priests had to sanctify themselves. No sanctification - no presence of God. No Presence of God - no genuine revival.

Then I want you to notice Exodus 19:6, *"And ye shall be unto me a kingdom of priests"* (KJV). God planned to make Israel a nation of priests. As a nation of priests, they would represent Him to the nations around them. They were to carry His Presence among them so that others would be drawn to Him. God wants you to carry His Presence into your world. The New Testament declaration of the same promise occurs in 1 Peter 2:9, *"But ye are a chosen generation, a royal priesthood, an holy nation, a peculiar people; that ye should shew forth the praises of him who hath called you out of darkness into his marvellous light"* (KJV).

We must become so full of His Presence that His fragrance drifts off us. Presence and information are not the same thing. You can be full of information and not be full of the Presence of God. Repentance (sanctification/consecration/holiness) must occur before His abiding Presence becomes a reality. One writer says "Esther spent six months soaking in oil of myrrh and six more months soaking in other added sweet odors to purify and prepare her for one night with the king. Can you imagine what Esther smelled like after spending a year soaking in the anointing oil? Everywhere she walked she left a cloud of incense." (Tommy Tenney, God's Favorite House, p 98-99).

When we become clean from sin to the place where His Presence soaks us, the world will smell the difference.

Key Number Three: Presence

Isaiah 64:1-5 *"Oh, that You would rend the heavens! That You would come down! That the mountains might shake at Your presence. As fire burns brushwood, As fire causes water to boil. To make Your name known to Your adversaries, That the nations may tremble at Your presence! When You did awesome things for which we did not look, You came down; The mountains shook at Your presence. For since the beginning of the world Men have not heard nor perceived by the ear, Nor has the eye seen any God besides You, Who acts for the one who waits for Him. You meet him who rejoices and does righteousness, who remembers You in Your ways. You are indeed angry, for we have sinned. In these ways, we continue, and we need to be saved."*

During the great Welsh revival this was a key passage of Scripture for Evan Roberts, the leader of the revival, who apparently prayed these verses on a regular basis. They contain both the third key to revival and to the types of things that place this key in our hands. Before examining this key of the manifest presence of God we perhaps should explore something of the difference between the manifest presence of God and the omnipresence of God.

Psalm 139 makes it clear God is omnipresent, that is, He is everywhere present at the same time. Scripture also makes it clear this omnipresent God can choose to manifest or reveal His presence in a tangible way. An example of this is seen in the account of Moses and the burning bush as described in Exodus chapter 3. God was always there, but He chose to reveal His Presence tangibly to Moses in the burning bush.

This manifest Presence of God is a major key to revival. In one sense it is the goal of revival, which is for us to know and walk in the awareness of His Glorious Presence. In another sense, it is this manifest Presence of God occurring in various regions that is a key to transforming those same regions. For example, in the days of Charles Finney, it was the manifest Presence of God that would come into a city that was often a key to that city turning to Jesus.

This manifest Presence of God brings with it five distinct blessings. First, it brings rest. The promise God gave Moses in Exodus 33:14 has to do with rest. *"And he said, My presence shall go with you, and I will give you rest"* (NKJV). Often in times of a manifested Presence of God people experience a sense of unusual rest. This may be an inner peace and calm. Sometimes when people encounter the Lord to the point where they fall to the floor, they experience that rest.

This manifest Presence of God will also bring joy. The Psalmist experienced this in Psalm 16:11, *"You will show me the path of life: in Your presence is fullness of joy; at your right hand are pleasures for evermore"* (NKJV). Revival historians have observed that people wondered why Evan Roberts laughed so much as he was preaching. His explanation of this was the joy he experienced in the Presence of the Lord.

Thirdly, this manifest presence of God brings a spiritual shelter. Psalm 31:20 records it this way, *"You shall hide them in the secret place of Your presence from the plots of man: You shall keep them secretly in a pavilion from the strife of tongues"* (NKJV). I call this "The feathered bomb shelter." This aspect of the manifest presence reminds me of the spokesman for a gospel quartet, who during a short season of intense revival, talked about not even wanting to go home because of the sense of shelter he was feeling in the service. Unkind things people say to us can often bring a great deal of hurt into our lives, but there is something about the manifest Presence of God that brings healing to those hurts.

A fourth blessing of the manifest presence of God is deliverance or salvation. The prophet Isaiah declared in Isaiah 63:9, *"In all their affliction he was afflicted, and the angel of his presence saved them: in his love and in his pity, he redeemed them, and he bore them and carried them all the days of old"* (NKJV). Jesus wants to be your savior, and Jesus wants to be your deliverer. Experience suggests that when a level of the manifest Presence of God comes, it brings an easier deliverance from demonic activity.

A final blessing of the manifest presence of God is refreshing. We read in Acts 3:19, *"Repent therefore and be converted, that your sins may be blotted out, so that times of refreshing may come from the presence of the Lord"* (NKJV). This may be the single most common testimony I hear when people encounter the manifest Presence of God. They feel so refreshed. Often words do not seem adequate to describe it. Most of Christian living still involves walking by faith, but we are invited to enter into times of refreshing. I notice in Acts 3:19 there is a link between the repenting and the refreshing.

Four words in the KJV refer to attracting this manifest

presence of God. The first of these is *"righteousness."* God meets or encounters those who work or do righteousness. Once again, this touches on the subject of holiness already written about in this chapter. I only add this thought. If holiness is important to God, then it must become important to me as well.

The second word describing what attracts God is *"rejoices."* This speaks to me of worship. Young's Literal Translation of this verse says *"Thou hast met with the rejoicer and the doer of righteousness."* There is something about worship from the heart that draws the manifest Presence of God. The thought is confirmed again in Psalm 22:3, *"But thou art holy, O thou that inhabitest the praises of Israel"* (KJV). Another word for "inhabit" is "dwell." (40% of the time the Hebrew word used here appears it is translated "dwell" in the KJV) I would suggest God dwells or resides where He is worshipped. Experience suggests most of the awesome times we encounter with the Lord's Presence come as His response to our worship of Him. Have you found this to be so? This is why the devil resists the worship of God so strongly.

Thirdly, the Lord is attracted to those who wait upon Him. Those who are wishing to encounter the awesome manifest Presence of God must understand you encounter this on His schedule and not on yours. I would suggest this is even more so if that Presence is to become a habitation. When your hunger for the Presence of God brings you to the point that everything else takes a back seat to that Presence and you lay things aside just for Him, you will be at a point where His manifest Presence will come. The Hebrew word used here includes the thought of "an attitude of earnest expectation and confident hope."

The final word in Isaiah chapter 64 is the word *"remember."* God meets with those who remember. To remember has the sense of "calling to mind." God often commanded people to build memorials so they would remember what He had done. This was not because He had forgotten, but it was because they needed to remember. The concept seems to be related to meditation. Scripture tells us to meditate on the following. You can meditate on the Lord; (how about the beauty of his holiness – Psalms 29:2 and 96:9). You can meditate on His Word. This includes the written Word of God. It also includes the Rhema Word of God to you. I encourage you to remember the promises God has given you. You can also meditate on His Work. This includes creation. I personally love to drive through the beautiful scenery of New Zealand just to bask in the beauty of His creation. This can also include the things God has done in your past. Tell the stories. I love to remember what God did in my life at Pensacola. I have learned in remembering the story or in telling it that it often stirs up that same manifest presence.

Before leaving this passage of Scripture, let me suggest that if these four things stir up the manifest Presence of God, then the opposite of them may well hinder that manifest presence. Sin in my life will stand as a barrier to the manifest Presence of God. I may get some of the overflow from others, but I will not experience the fullness myself. The more sin there is in the church, the more difficult it is to get into the manifest Presence of God. This does not imply that the presence of sinners in a meeting will limit what God does. I have seen witches attempt unsuccessfully to take over a meeting or attempt some level of mind control. That can be overcome. I am talking about the basic church. God gives grace where sinners are involved (especially in evangelistic moments), but He requires more of His people.

A lack of worship will stand as a barrier to the manifest presence of God. Some worship, but do not live holy lives. They rarely encounter the genuine manifest presence of God. Others are holy but, they are not worshippers. They, too, rarely encounter that genuine manifest Presence of God. Those who do not worship will not experience God. There is a major difference between looking at a tiger track and looking a tiger in the eye. I heard Leonard Ravenhill say on an audio tape that most people go to church to learn about God, but not to meet Him.

The third barrier to the manifest Presence of God is busy-ness.

For many of us, this is the big culprit. We are too busy to take time for the Lord. The day slips away, and we have not spent time with Him. We rush through a worship service, anxiously waiting for it to end because we have other things we want or need to do.

And then forgetfulness becomes a hindrance. Don't forget His promises to you. Don't forget what He has done. His presence can become a habitation.

For even more on this, I have a complete chapter comparing the anointing, the manifest Presence of God, and the Glory of God in my book The Glory Factor.

Key Number Four: Humility

Humility is essential if we are to please God. We are told in Micah 6:8 that God requires us to *"walk humbly with thy God."* Indeed, God promises blessings for the humble. In Psalm 10:17 God promises to hear the prayer or desire of the humble. In Matthew 5:5 Jesus said, *"they shall inherit the earth."* Strong's concordance says by implication the word translated *"meek"* in Matthew 5:5 carries the thought of "humility." Another promise is found in James 4:6, *"God ...giveth grace unto the humble."* 1 Peter 5:6 promises they will *"be exalted in due time."*

Humility is also directly related to revival. It is a pre-requisite for lasting revival. King Josiah came to the throne during a time of great wickedness in the lives of God's people. Fifty-seven years of ungodly leadership had just concluded, and judgment had been pronounced upon the land, but because of things found in the heart of Josiah a reprieve was granted. Consider what the Lord said in 2 Kings 22:19, *"Because thine heart was tender, and thou hast humbled thyself before the LORD, when thou heardest what I spake against this place, and against the inhabitants thereof, that they should become a desolation and a curse, and hast rent thy clothes, and wept before me; I also have heard thee, saith the LORD"* (KJV). Did you catch it? Josiah had a heart after God. When he became aware of sin, he simply repented. No excuses were offered. The humility spoken of was demonstrated by his actions. His tender heart became broken over the sin he saw and the judgment that was to come. I submit that revival will not come to our lives and churches until we humble ourselves.

Not only is it a pre-requisite for revival but humility also brings healing into the land of the humble. Few verses are more familiar to those people longing for revival than 2 Chronicles 7:14, *"If my people, which are called by my name, shall humble themselves, and pray, and seek my face, and turn from their wicked ways; then will I hear from heaven, and will forgive their sin, and will heal their land"* (KJV). Humility is one of the four ingredients of revival described in this text. The others are prayer, the seeking of God's face, and the turning away from sin.

To humble oneself is to bend the knee. It is pictured by the vanquished army on its knees with head bowed before the victor. We do not come to God on equal terms; rather we must come to Him in surrender. There can be no friendship until first of all there is Lordship. I heard it reported that during the War of 1812 the commander of a defeated ship stepped onto the deck of his conqueror with his hand outstretched. His outstretched hand was greeted with this statement, "Your sword first, sir." Friendship can be established. In fact, God desires to be our friend, but the relationship involves my humble submission to Him first.

It is the very opposite of the proud, arrogant person. Remember that Jesus said the humble publican was received while the proud Pharisee was rejected in the sight of God.

One of the key moments of the Welsh revival occurred when Evan Roberts began to respond to the thought of "bend me." Indeed, this became one of his prayers. This is humility. Someone observed you could only get to heaven on bended knee. Experience has taught me arrogance will bring an end to the move of God. Revival movements will lose it when they become impressed with their own record. Will you join me in rejecting the spirit of independence?

Let's tell God how much we need Him. It seems to me it is time for the church to recognize that our present methods are not working, so humility calls us to try His instead.

Finally, humility brings the presence of God. *"For thus saith the high and lofty One that inhabiteth eternity, whose name is Holy; I dwell in the high and holy place, with him also that is of a contrite and humble spirit, to revive the spirit of the humble, and to revive the heart of the contrite ones"* (Isaiah 57:15, KJV). God declares He has two places of habitation. First, He dwells in the high and holy place. He lives in eternity. That is a concept beyond my pay grade. But He also dwells with *"him of a contrite and humble spirit."* Wow! May I suggest humility is a key to the presence of God sweeping in and remaining? This is a lifestyle of brokenness, for the word *"contrite"* has to do with being crushed. Will you let God crush your heart that He may live in it? Did you notice the promise God made? He revives the heart of the humble and contrite. The humble heart can become a revived heart.

Key Number Five: Harvest

The evangelist in me loves to rise up and declare harvest is the result of revival. Indeed, the evangelist in me can passionately declare, if there is no harvest there is no revival, for every genuine revival will have a harvest of souls. We believe it is the heart of God to send revival that brings in the harvest. As precious as renewal and refreshing are we must move deeper. We must feel the heart of God for the lost. This is not to suggest we should rush or force a harvest before the time is right. Seed time still precedes harvest time.

But let me suggest revival is maintained as we keep a focus on the lost. It is a deeply held conviction in my heart that if we allow revival to be focused on self, we will lose it. One of my former professors expressed it as being spiritual navel gazers. I thank God for the blessings we receive from the Lord, but these blessings are not for our benefit only. God wants to touch others through us. The power of God we crave to flow through us will not flow if it is for us only. We are reminded in Mark 10:45, *"For even the Son of Man came not to be ministered unto but to minister"* (KJV). I stress frequently we must receive before we can give; this is a Biblical principle. But having received, we must pass it on.

Isaiah 66:5-9 is one of the great Scriptural promises of the harvest that is going to come. *"Hear the word of the LORD, you who tremble at his word; 'Your brothers who hate you, and exclude you because of my name, have said, 'Let the LORD be glorified, that we may see your joy!' Yet they will be put to shame. Hear that uproar from the city, hear that noise from the temple! It is the sound of the LORD repaying his enemies all they deserve. 'Before she goes into labour, she gives birth; before the pains come upon her, she delivers a son.' Who has ever heard of such a thing? Who has ever seen such things? Can a country be born in a day or a nation be brought forth in a moment? Yet no sooner is Zion in labor than she gives birth to her children. 'Do I bring to the moment of birth and not give delivery?' says the LORD. 'Do I close up the womb when I bring to delivery?' says your God"* (NIV).

The enemies of God were mocking God's people. Indeed, they are said to have hated and excluded them, but God had a word for the situation. Judgment was going to fall on those who resisted Him and lived in rebellion, and an outpouring was going to occur. As soon as travail occurs the birth would happen. We are talking about rapid conversions! So many would get saved it would be as if the earth was born in one day or as if an entire nation came into being in one day. Then God promises to give strength for the birth to occur. This passage is such an encouragement to me. A great harvest of souls is on God's agenda.

This harvest may have seasons to it, for Jeremiah 5:24 reads, *"...Let us fear the LORD our God, who gives autumn and spring rains in season, who assures us of the regular weeks of harvest"* (NIV). Just as God has planned for natural seasons of harvest, He also sends spiritual seasons of harvest. Friend, when God sends such a season don't miss it. I have seen evidence suggesting some churches have missed a season. In the first few days of what became a nineteen-week visitation from God to a church, a former leader of the church urged them not to miss what God was doing. He said, "Eleven years ago God tried to do this in our midst, and we missed Him. Let's not miss Him this time." They had been so busy with their good agenda that they had missed God's agenda. Thank God most of them caught the second chance.

Joel 2:23-24 confirms this thought of seasons in revival. *"Be glad, O people of Zion, rejoice in the LORD your God, for he has given you the autumn rains in righteousness. He sends you abundant showers, both autumn and spring rains, as before. The threshing-floors will be filled with grain; the vats will overflow with new wine and oil"* (NIV). Not only are there seasons in revival but God wants to send the rain so that the harvest floors (threshing floors) will be full; they will overflow. Rain is always required for a harvest. For too long the church has tried to have a dry harvest. We have tried to bring about a harvest without rain from heaven. Without the rain, there is no growth. Some need to read this paragraph again and meditate on it. This verse is another support for the WOW being connected to the OOHH of the second chapter.

Jesus repeatedly declared He sees the harvest as abundant. In Matthew 9:37 *"the harvest truly is plenteous"* while in Luke 10:2, it *"truly is great."* Jesus urged His disciples to *"look on the fields; for they are white already to harvest"* (John 4:35). In Mark 4:29 He said, *"the harvest is come."* In Matthew 13:39 Jesus connects the harvest to *"the end of the age."* A last day's revival will have much harvest as a part of it.

But while the harvest is promised a partnership is required to bring it to pass. Jesus called His disciples to first become partners in prayer in Matthew 9:37-38, *"Then he said to his disciples, 'The harvest is plentiful, but the workers are few. Ask the Lord of the harvest, therefore, to send out workers into his harvest field'"* (NIV). Revival evangelism and revival intercession should be linked together.

Psalm 126:6 should be a great encouragement to the weeping revivalist. *"He who goes out weeping, carrying seed to sow, will return with songs of joy, carrying sheaves with him."* We pray in the harvest. This continues to be true even during revival. This principle is revealed again in James 5:18, *"Again he prayed, and the heavens gave rain, and the earth produced its crops"* (NIV). I believe the burden for intercession for the lost must grip our hearts as it never has before. Only those churches who take hold of this and understand the importance of praying in the harvest will see the harvest. Unless someone prays it in it will not happen. We can have little church games and little church activities, but we will not shake the gates of hell. I believe it is too late for us to play little games now, We must enter the arena and contend for our cities. If you do not contend for your city, who will?

This partnership will not stop with the prayer closet. Labor will be involved. There is work in this harvest. Once we have prayed it through we must go out in the power of the Spirit into the world where God has placed us. Revival can be spelled W-O-R-K. During a fifteen-week revival in northern Indiana, I stepped into the pastor's office on a Sunday morning when he was still working on sermon notes. As I entered his office, he said, "I was never like this before revival came. I always had all the messages for Sunday done by Friday." However, the work load had increased because of revival. I remember walking into his office on another occasion to see a line of eleven people waiting to see him. Many of the new converts needed counseling. The revival service was fun, but discipleship was work.

God's Word proclaims, *"He who gathers crops in summer is a wise son, but he who sleeps during harvest is a disgraceful son"* (Proverbs 10:5). Are we wise sons or are we asleep? I preached a seven-week meeting in the revival of the 90s where approximately 250 responded to a salvation invitation. The pastor observed almost every sinner that came into the auditorium made his or her way to the altar for salvation. He challenged his church on a Sunday morning to bring the lost. He even suggested some had not been honest with him. They told him they wanted to see the lost saved, but their actions did not indicate the same. He was trying to motivate them to take advantage of the season God had given them.

Jesus challenged His disciples in John 4:35, *"Do you not say, 'Four months more and then the harvest'? I tell you, open your eyes and look at the fields! They are ripe for harvest."* The harvest is still waiting for someone to gather it in. Will you gather the harvest around your city? Now is not the time to faint. As Galatians 6:9 says, *"Let us not become weary in doing good, for at the proper time we will reap a harvest if we do not give up."* Let us go after the harvest more than ever before. I call you to renew every effort...spare no energy...use every financial resource you can. Just get the harvest in!

Failing to partner in a harvest can put the harvest in peril. For the church, the great peril is the harvest could go from a plentiful harvest to becoming a spoiled harvest. The prophet writes in Joel 1:11, *"Despair, you farmers, wail, you vine growers; grieve for the wheat and the barley because the harvest of the field is destroyed."* In God's judgment on His people, the harvest was lost. Is it possible the spiritual harvest of the field is about to perish? Jeremiah 8:20 warns us, *"The harvest is past, the summer has ended, and we are not saved."* What a tragedy for the church to go and seek to bring in the harvest only to discover the time of opportunity is no longer available. The Spirit is no longer brooding as He once was. We had a season, and we lost it. This is a sad testimony, but it can happen. We preached a month-long revival in a midwestern community. Over 70 people responded to the work of the Spirit drawing them to Jesus. Years later a new pastor was being interviewed by the church. He was told, "We experienced the greatest revival in the history of the church with the Livengoods. However, we lost it." Another pastor told me his church decided they loved the WOW of revival but did not want to engage with the OOHH. Emotional times in His presence were loved, but they had not translated into a passion for the lost. The revival that had come did not last. They were discovering the Presence would not remain when they were not ready to labor in the harvest field.

Finally, this harvest cannot be accomplished by our power. We must embrace the power of the harvest. Isn't it interesting that before releasing the apostles to go and make disciples of all nations Jesus commanded them to return to Jerusalem? They were to remain there until they had been filled with the Holy Spirit. Luke 24:49 contains these instructions, *"Behold, I send the Promise of My Father upon you; but tarry in the city of Jerusalem until you are endued with power from on high."* Again, Jesus makes His desires clear in Acts 1:8, *"But you shall receive power when the Holy Spirit has come upon you; and you shall be witnesses to Me in Jerusalem, and in all Judea and Samaria, and to the end of the earth."*

"The sower soweth the word. And these are they by the way side, where the word is sown; but when they have heard, Satan cometh immediately, and taketh away the word that was sown in their hearts. And these are they likewise which are sown on stony ground; who, when they have heard the word, immediately receive it with gladness; And have no root in themselves, and so endure but for a time: afterward, when affliction or persecution ariseth for the word's sake, immediately they are offended. And these are they which are sown among thorns; such as hear the word, And the cares of this world, and the deceitfulness of riches, and the lusts of other things entering in, choke the word, and it becometh unfruitful. And these are they which are sown on good ground; such as hear the word, and receive it, and bring forth fruit, some thirtyfold, some sixty, and some an hundred." Mark 4:14-20

4

DO NOT ABORT THE REVIVAL

A well-known revivalist tells of pleading with God to send revival to the nation. His fervent prayer was interrupted by a question posed to Him by God. "Do you know how many revivals I start every year?"

The issue often is not "How can we get God to come to our church?" Rather what needs to be done so we do not abort a revival before it is fully birthed?

In 1996 the Lord God most sovereignly and graciously walked my wife and me into revival. That season has continued from that day to this. In this chapter and the one to follow I want to focus on the principles He taught us in the early days of revival.

Speaking of principles, one of the first things He spoke to me about was the necessity of living by principles. Often during the first flush of revival, we can be so caught up in the drama of it that we begin to live off spiritual adrenalin, but that cannot be sustained. The principles of God's Word must be the patterns we live by. If they are followed, we will be able to navigate the white waters of revival. If we fail to live by His principles, we will probably turn our boat upside down on them.

We were still in the early days of revival, the days of wonder, the days of the WOW, when the Lord began to deal with me about not aborting revival. Many of the sermons I have preached over the years were put together with a lot of work. I have had to sweat over the passage of Scripture and then struggle to put together an outline that would express what I felt the Lord was trying to communicate, but the material for this chapter did not come that way. Let me explain.

We were preaching what became a two-week meeting in the suburbs of Chicago. The pastor had called for a day of fasting and prayer with a corporate time of prayer at the noon hour. During the time we were praying, I was pacing up and down an aisle in the auditorium which was a rather normal thing for me to do. Somehow my attention was drawn to Mark 4:13-20 which is the parable of the seed and the sower. It seemed as if the Lord replaced the word, *"word"* in the text with the word *"revival."* Suddenly the passage became a sound from heaven for me. For the next few years, I felt led by the Lord to share from this passage at every revival we preached. Let me print the passage in its entirety.

"Then Jesus said to them, "Don't you understand this parable? How then will you understand any parable? The farmer sows the word. Some people are like seed along the path, where the word is sown. As soon as they hear it, Satan comes and takes away the word that was sown in them. Others, like seed sown on rocky places, hear the word and at once receive it with joy. But since they

have no root, they last only a short time. When trouble or persecution comes because of the word, they quickly fall away. Still others, like seed sown among thorns, hear the word; but the worries of this life, the deceitfulness of wealth and the desires for other things come in and choke the word, making it unfruitful. Others, like seed sown on good soil, hear the word, accept it, and produce a crop - thirty, sixty or even a hundred times what was sown." Mark 4:13-20 (NIV)

Satan Steals Revival

Satan will always try to steal your revival. *"As soon as they hear it Satan comes and takes away."* The KJV uses the word *"immediately."* I write this chapter less than 40 hours after finishing a camp for men on the South Island of New Zealand. The day the camp ended I spoke at a church in a nearby city. Some of the men who had been in the camp attended this service. One asked me, "How do we sustain what God did at the camp?" He observed that just a few hours after leaving that spiritually charged atmosphere and stepping back into the "real world" it almost felt as if the camp had never happened.

Satan's strategy has always included stealing from you what God has done in your life. If he cannot keep you from receiving from the Lord, then he will try to keep you from keeping what God has given you. It is possible to leave a powerful service only to walk directly into an attempt by the devil to take away what God has done. My father described such an attempt in his early days as a Christian. He and the people in the church he attended walked out of a great evening service to discover that someone had slashed two tires on every car in the church parking area. The Satanic strategy was meant to undermine what God had just done in the service.

The devil often says two things about revival. First, he will say "The revival was not real." He will say "The revival was not from God." I have watched people talk themselves out of something God did for them. If they do not talk themselves out of it, somebody else will tell them what they experienced was not of God. I recall a meeting in a church in 1996 that had a huge impact on a young couple. They entered in enthusiastically and were powerfully ministered to by the Holy Spirit. A couple of weeks into the revival one set of their parents, whose theological background rejected the events of the revival, began to tell this young couple the revival was not from God. Sadly, they successfully talked the young couple out of the revival.

Satan Persecutes Revival

The second thing the devil will say is, "The revival won't last. It will only be temporary." He may concede the revival happened. However, he will suggest it will not continue. As a pastor, I became aware one of my older "saints" was encouraging a younger believer not to associate with a certain new Christian because he would never last, and we did not want him in our church. We can become so convinced a revival can only be temporary that we look for signs of its exit as soon as it enters.

If Satan cannot talk you out of a revival, he will persecute it. This persecution will often begin with a direct spiritual oppression, which usually comes as an attack on your mind. If this direct spiritual oppression does not work, your flesh may rebel against certain aspects of the revival. During the Brownsville revival, my wife experienced this. While we were attending services, our attention was drawn to some who were "shaking." Linda did not have an issue per se with people shaking under the power of God. However, there were some aspects of it that concerned her. During that season she had an encounter with the Lord where He asked if He could shake her? She realized it was a serious question. She was face to face with her willingness to allow the Spirit of God to take her where she had not been before. In that sense, Linda's flesh was struggling, and she had to decide how she would respond.

Do Not Abort the Revival

A third way Satan may try to persecute your revival will come through the opinion of others. Your friends and family may think you are crazy. Pentecostals have long faced these kinds of charges. In saying this, I am not encouraging activity that is outside the bounds of Scripture. Rather, it is to recognize that revival can be controversial. Even those closest to us may not understand it. Scripture tells us that even the brothers of Jesus did not believe in Him (see John 7:5).

It is possible your church may not like it. Those who have experienced and embraced revival find it hard to believe that the church may reject it, but the truth is that it does happen. I was the preacher of a meeting that became a powerful revival for the church and area. However, within a year, the deacons' board of the church indicated to its pastor it did not want to see revival continue.

A friend pastored a church when the most significant revival of its history occurred. In a city that once won the dubious award of the crime capital of the United States and was known for its racism revival broke out. Members of both the black and white community wept together at the altar. Scores of people came into the Kingdom of God including a man with mafia connections. The crowds that came outgrew the auditorium. Yet after seventeen weeks of this amazing move of God a petition came from certain members of the church asking that the revival meetings be closed.

Revival may be embraced by the city in which it occurs, but in other cases, cities have rejected a move of God. In some cases, your community may even despise you. Such resistance to the move of God should not surprise us.

Satan Diverts Revival

Third, if Satan cannot stop a revival by persecuting it, then he will try to divert your revival. How does he do this?

Three things are suggested in Mark chapter 4. First, diversion comes through the cares of this life. We can become so occupied with good stuff that we miss out on the important stuff. Distraction has often brought revival to a halt. Life happens. Even during great moves of God certain practical things need to be taken care of. Dishes still need to be washed. Laundry will need to be done. People will still have to go to work…school…and so forth. I well remember a conversation with a friend out of the Brownsville revival. He described the early weeks of that revival where they would leave the service as the sun was rising to go to work. After work, they would grab a meal and head off for church. I had to ask some questions? When did you sleep? When did you buy groceries? When did you do laundry or mow your lawn? Somehow those things got done. The constant battle is between balancing the concerns of the Kingdom and the cares of life.

Revival can also be diverted by the deceitfulness of riches. The desire for success and prosperity can become center stage in our lives and crowd out revival. Have you ever noticed how many people get job transfers when God starts moving in their life? Certainly, we believe God desires to bless us in every area of our life, but we also understand that even the blessing can become a curse. The deception of riches can impact a revival in many ways. Some will miss revival because their desire for wealth and what it provides becomes more important than the revival. For others, greed destroys revival in quite a different way. Sometimes revival produces significant income for those in the revival, and the temptation is to use revival for financial advantage.

Both the text and experience suggest revival can be distracted because of lust. Please understand - revival will not remove your humanity. Temptation, including sexual temptation, will still happen. More than one revival has been shut down by the moral failure of one of its leaders. A very famous revival in a southern state came to an early demise because the evangelist was having an affair.

In the late 1990s, while preaching at a church in the southern USA, I became aware the people seemed hesitant to respond to the altar time. They responded, but at the same time "hung back." When

I finally asked the pastor what happened at this church to create such a distrust toward revival preachers, he told me a previous pastor had been powerfully touched by a national revival. The anointing of that revival seemed to spill into this church, leading to a great season of God. However, after a few weeks of revival, it was discovered that the pastor was having an affair with the wife of his youth pastor. This moral failure totally devastated the church and created a huge suspicion toward revival.

Satan Limits Revival

Satan's next strategy will be to try to limit your harvest. If he cannot stop the revival from happening…if he cannot talk you out of it…if he cannot grind it to a halt through persecution…if he cannot successfully distract it, then he will simply try to limit its effectiveness. He will try to limit the number getting saved. He will try to stop the sanctification it is creating. He will do this in all or any of three ways. The first of these is spiritual pride. This is the mindset that says; we have arrived and do not need any more of Him. I was part of a multi-week revival that probably ended too soon. At one point, I stumbled upon some of the youth discussing the revival. Pridefully they were discussing the fact they were THE church in the valley experiencing revival. In their opinion, no one else was experiencing revival. As I listened to the conversation, I felt a grieving in my spirit. My concern was a spirit of pride would bring an end to the move of God. It did. A friend preached there scarcely a year later and described that church as one of the deadest churches he had ever preached in. Pride still precedes destruction (Proverbs 16:18).

Another strategy of Satan to limit revival is spiritual complacency. We become comfortable with things as they are; we do not want the river to get deeper. Revival will always push our complacency boundaries. Sometimes people enter into revival and find challenges they did not expect. Ezekiel chapter 47 describes a river that flows from the altar of God that has different depths to it. It begins at the ankles, rises to the knees, then it reaches the loins. Finally, it becomes a river to swim in. I have watched people determining which levels they were comfortable with. Some were content to stop at the ankles, while others wanted to go deeper. Let me be clear. God's love for us is not determined by which level of revival we are content with. Tragically, we limit the possibilities revival can produce when we become complacent at a particular depth of the river. Some enjoy the new freedom revival brings, but do not want it to change the structure of their church or their personal lives.

A third strategy to limiting revival is spiritual instability. If spiritual complacency causes you to stop at a particular depth of the river, spiritual instability makes the revivalist weird. The one captured by spiritual instability will focus more on the manifestation than on God. They begin looking for the gift more than for the Giver. They are tempted to create by human effort what can only come from God. We must not let revival become idolatrous. We must love and seek Jesus even more than revival.

Each of these attempts of Satan to abort revival can be drawn from the parable of the sower.

I want to mention two more of his strategies to abort revival that are not in the parable but are ones I have observed. Revival will have costs and changes. First, it will cost the revivalist. There is a spiritual cost in carrying revival anointing, but that is not the cost I want to consider at this point. The revivalist will experience personal costs in reputation. Not everyone will understand revival. Some will question your motives and integrity. During a meeting in an Indiana community, I was praying with people at the altar who wanted "more" of God in their lives. I had been gently touching people on the foreheads as I prayed for them. Most of them were falling to the floor under the power of the Spirit of God. I approached one man, whom I later discovered was a police officer, to pray for him. My hand was about an inch from his forehead when

I felt forbidden by the Holy Spirit to touch him. Now, I am reasonably sure that even with his eyes closed he could sense my hand close to his head, but I never touched him. As I was standing there trying to decide what to do next, he fell to the floor. Again, I never touched him! When he got to his feet, he immediately told others I had pushed him. When they indicated I had not done so, he became adamant that he had felt me push him. Even when 20 or more persons indicated they could bear witness that I had not touched him he still maintained I had pushed him because he felt it. To this day he believes I pushed him. Nothing can change his mind. My motives and integrity are not highly regarded by him. By the way, I do believe it is possible someone pushed him, but it was just not me!

On another occasion, I was shaking hands with people as I was making my way to my seat at the beginning of the service. We had just concluded the pre-service prayer time. We were in the first week of what became a seven-week revival. As I went to shake hands with one man, he indicated he would not shake my hand. He indicated that he had seen what I had done to that boy on Sunday and that I was a charlatan. He told me I had brought confusion to the church, and he was there to rebuke me in the Lord. To this day I am not certain who the young man was, nor am I aware of what I did. I only know he thought I was a charlatan, which was an experience I do not recommend.

I am also aware that my acceptance of revival has cost me some pulpits. One invitation was withdrawn when the pastor knew I was "a Brownsville person."

Finally, revival will produce changes. It will produce changes within us. I had to learn to flow and guide but not try to control. Some church wineskins will change. For me, the risks of revival paled in comparison with the value of it. As for me and my house, based on solid, Pentecostal, Biblical foundations, we decided just to let the wind blow!

And my, how the wind has blown!

5

STOKING THE FIRES OF REVIVAL

"Where no wood is, there the fire goeth out." – Pr 26:20

When a revival that would ultimately run for fifteen weeks broke open at an Indiana congregation, the pastor asked me to join him in tag team teaching a Sunday school class. The purpose of the class was to help people deal with the fire of revival.

Proverbs 26:20-21 became our springboard. It says, *"Where no wood is, there the fire goeth out: so where there is no talebearer, the strife ceaseth. As coals are to burning coals, and wood to fire; so is a contentious man to kindle strife"* (KJV). We knew the thrust of those two verses was and is a warning against gossip. However, we saw a principle contained within them that relates to revival. The fires of revival must be stoked!

Have you ever attempted to keep a campfire going? If a campfire is going to continue to burn it needs two things. First, it needs oxygen, and secondly, it needs fuel. You must keep wood on the fire, or it will go out. Those verses in Proverbs recognize that. We understood revival fire had been ignited in the hearts of many in the church, so our question centered around "What must be done to keep that fire burning?" We believed it was the will of God for those fires to continue to burn within the hearts and lives of those in that church. We believed it was God's will for them to continue to burn within the church itself. We believed if we could keep the individual fires burning the corporate fire would naturally keep burning as well.

The focus of this chapter will be to share with you some of the practical steps we shared with that church over a six-week period on how to keep the fire of revival burning.

We understood the source of oxygen for that revival fire was the wind of the Spirit, and He would do His part. Our part would be to keep the fuel for revival fresh. We had to keep stoking the fire. Here are some principles we found necessary to do that.

Do Not Stop at Maintenance Mentality

Have you ever watched an athletic team get so consumed with protecting its lead they stopped doing the things that got them the lead and ultimately lost the game?

I suggest we be less concerned about maintenance and more concerned about expansion. We must be less concerned about holding onto what God gave us and more concerned about giving it away to others.

Two things are essential in developing your marriage. The first is that you keep courting your spouse. The second is communication. In a successful marriage, both husband and wife understand they must keep working at the marriage. Marriages can drift apart if the couple does not continue to do the things that keep their marriage strong. They value the relationship. They value each other. They keep talking to each other. Have you ever noticed the couple that can talk for hours at a time before they get married sometimes get married and then suddenly they cannot find anything to talk about?

These principles are true for spiritual relationships as well. As the bride of Christ, I must value my relationship with Him. As the bride of Christ, I must take the time to communicate with Him.

Revival may have the sovereign "suddenly moment," but it also has intentionality to it. I make it a priority in my life. I prepare to set aside time to be in God's House. Things of the Kingdom remain a priority for me.

In a strong marriage, the couple knows what their partner likes. The focus becomes how I can please my spouse. Giving becomes more important than taking. In sustaining revival, I become more concerned about what pleases my Heavenly Groom than in what I am receiving. The more partners invest in the relationship, the more they receive from that relationship.

Understand the Changes Must be Permanent

Revival will always bring change to a church. It will always bring change to the life of the revived. We must understand those changes must be permanent. The Biblical principle is "new wineskins for the new wine." In revival, it is not unusual that a certain percentage of the people will always wonder, "When will we go back to the way it used to be?" Some just want "their church" to be the way it was. They want the services to remain the same length. They want the weekly schedule to look the same. However, the reality is that some old programs may need to be given a decent funeral service. We must remember that principles never change but methods may. Indeed, some methods must change to accommodate what God is doing.

Not only will revival produce change within a church it will produce change within a person. If you want to keep the fire burning in your heart, you must understand you cannot go back to the old life. This means you must be done with sin. Sin revealed by the Spirit and then repented of must not be resumed. In practice, this may mean some TV programs and lifestyle patterns will need to change.

In the early days of revival, I noticed an interesting

phenomenon. Because services were running night after night and were often running late into the night television time became more limited. As the revival progressed, we began to take "break" nights to avoid wearing the people out and to make room for the other things in life that needed to be done. Some would flip the TV on during those break nights, and it was not unusual for some to feel TV had somehow changed. Suddenly the language seemed coarse and the scenes racier. Of course, the reality was that television had not changed in those few weeks but the person watching had changed. Things we would never have noticed before now grated on our spirits the way finger nails being scraped across a chalkboard would grate on our physical ears. However, it is possible to once again become dull of spiritual sense. Slowly we can pick up all the habits and routines that dulled our spiritual sensitivity before the revival.

Permanent change involves more than what we stop doing. We begin to add new things to our lives. Time is allotted for the development of the life of God within us. Our daily devotional life begins to change. We find a burning desire to spend more time with Him. That flame must be stoked! Fifteen minutes is not enough. Now we need at least 30 to 60 minutes of daily fellowship with Him. Attendance at church becomes more consistent. We hate to miss the meeting because we know He is going to be there. Priorities are adjusted to reflect our new reality. We love going to church now. You feel David's passion in Psalm 122:1, *"I was glad when they said unto me, Let us go into the house of the LORD."* Before revival, you were hoping for a short sermon and a short service because you had things you needed to do. Now you feel cheated if the service is too short and the sermon is more like a sermonette. You start scanning the newspaper to see if special services are being held on the "off nights" in an area church.

I even noticed when revival broke in churches the types of things being purchased at the resource table changed. People began buying more worship CDs and preaching/teaching sets and fewer cute tee shirts. This change was simply a reflection of their new priorities. More and more concern was now being given to developing the spirit person living inside of their bodies. Now they were going after God.

Keep Going After God

Often during the days of the Brownsville revival Evangelist Steve Hill would exhort the church to keep going after God. But what does that mean?

Certainly, it included the way we entered the service itself. Half-hearted participation was not going after God. Worship became more intense. During prayer ministry, time to go after God included getting into the prayer line. We looked for those wearing a prayer team badge and requested they pray for us. Sometimes we would get prayed for several times a night. We lingered at the altar until the darkening of the auditorium lights required us to leave. Even this level of going after God must be cultivated. I found I had to overcome spiritual inertia to receive prayer. It was easy to simply become a spectator rather than a participator. I could quite easily stand on the steps leading to the balcony and watch others receiving. And it is not wrong to watch others getting blessed. A secondary or spill over blessing is available. These could also be times of learning how to move and minister. However, these spectator moments often degenerate into spiritual complacency. I could become content just watching. I had to force myself to participate. Spiritual osmosis was not enough. I had to go after God myself. But for revival to sustain going after God takes on a larger meaning.

Here are four things going after God came to mean for me. First, I had to develop a Kingdom heart. The concerns of the Kingdom of God had to be more important than the concerns of my personal kingdom. Scripture admonishes me *"seek ye first the kingdom"* (Matthew 6:33). I needed to join in the prayer Jesus prayed in Matthew 6:10, *"Thy Kingdom come."* I found a new emphasis from Romans 14:17, *"The Kingdom of God is not meat...but righteousness...peace...joy."* I urge you to keep going after God, to make His Kingdom paramount.

Secondly, intercessory prayer became a priority. I heard Dick Eastman teach at a "Change the World School of Prayer" that intercessory prayer is love on its knees. This type of prayer identifies with God's concerns. It becomes more focused on the advance of the Kingdom of God. Intercessory prayer seems to become more important in revival. If prayer was a vital element in attracting the Presence of God, it is just as vital to retaining it. Not all will have an intercessor's ministry, but all must intercede. If you want revival to be sustained in your church, then elevate prayer in the church. If you want sustained revival in your life, do the same thing. Sometimes intercession is hard work. I have described it as blood and guts and tears and snot. It is not always pretty, but it sustains revival.

For me, the third element in going after God is evangelism. We must have a heart for people. Rivers turned inward become stagnant ponds. Rivers turned outward continue to flow with fresh water. Keep witnessing. Keep inviting people to church. Learn more about soul winning. Pray for God to give you His heart for souls. Stir your own heart for the same. Look for opportunities to pray for people in the public arena. Even before revival, I observed that often the people in a church who were the most alive were those sharing their faith.

A fourth element of going after God is doing works of service. Jonathan Edwards wrote in 1746 in "A Treatise Concerning Religious Affections" that a full-fledged revival will involve a balance between personal concern for individuals and social concerns. He was convinced that religious meetings, prayer, singing, and religious talk will not promote or sustain revival in the absence of works of love and mercy, which will "bring the God of love down from heaven to earth." Real revival affects our Christian works as James 2:18 says faith is reflected in works. I have noticed the churches that seem to sustain revival are often the ones that have made outreach and evangelism a priority.

Watch for the Snares

Some make the mistake of believing that an outpouring of the Spirit removes all temptation. Do not be deceived by that thinking. In his excellent book "Feast of Fire" John Kilpatrick lists several snares that will come along in revival.

Temptation to fail morally may occur during revival. Your flesh is not dead yet, so you must learn to walk in wisdom. For many years I served as the camp dean for my denomination's youth camps. As a part of my responsibility, I helped guide the counselors during the week. Often on the morning before the last service, I talked to the counselors about temptations that students would face on that last night. I talked about the expected move of God in the evening service. I explained how students encountering the love of God would also want to express that love to someone else. Of itself that is a good thing. However, what begins in the Spirit can slip over into the flesh. So, we talked about appropriate and inappropriate expressions of brotherly and sisterly love. We gave counsel to the leaders regarding ways to monitor and encourage appropriate expressions of love and how to intervene if they saw expressions that were not appropriate. I grew up singing a song that included the phrase, "standing somewhere in the shadows you will find Jesus." I would tell the counselors the only people I wanted in the shadows were counselors - with flashlights! I did not want some young person full of the love of Jesus to be moved from Spirit to flesh with improper sexual activity being the result. I am attempting to be careful in what I write here, but immorality can arise in the middle of a move of God. I am tragically aware of a pastor's wife who became emotionally and sexually involved with a male intercessor while her husband was away preaching. The nightly prayer encounters became more than that. Your flesh is not dead yet, so you need to set boundaries on yourself.

Another snare is the temptation to be critical. In the middle of revival, you can face the temptation to criticize those who are "not in the river." Satan loves to divide a revival into those who are "more spiritual" and those who are "less spiritual." We can criticize those who do not worship the way we do. We can criticize those who have not entered into the revival as we have.

Sometimes we face temptation to criticize leadership because now we know more than they do. During revivals, I have often pled with visitors not to return to their churches and criticize them because they were not experiencing the same revival. I have sat down with pastors who were being criticized by members of their church for not being spiritual...or not being led by the Spirit...or not being people of faith. The list goes on and on.

Sometimes we can be tempted to criticize things we do not understand about revival. I believe I should be able to give Biblical foundation for the activities of revival. This is a truth supported by the apologists' favorite verse in Scripture, *"But sanctify the Lord God in your hearts: and be ready always to give an answer to every man that asketh you a reason of the hope that is in you with meekness and fear"* (1 Peter 3:15). But I must also understand that God may not feel obligated to explain all His ways to me.

A third snare which the revivalist needs to be leery of is the temptation to pride. If he cannot keep you out of the river of revival the devil will try to puff you up. More than one revivalist has discovered the painful reality of Proverbs 16:18, *"Pride goeth before destruction, and an haughty spirit before a fall."* (KJV) I must never become too impressed with myself. He does not need me, and I cannot survive without Him.

Another extreme is the snare of spiritual weirdness. Perhaps you know someone who flipped out or is strange. A family member was pastoring a church that was experiencing some small level of revival when one of the men heard a voice he thought came from God telling him to go and march around the local school and claim it for God. It is one thing to go after hours and pray over a local school. It is entirely another thing to trespass on school property during school hours. His misguided zeal served to bring confusion into his own life and fear into the church. Often this fear keeps many from going after God.

So, how do you stay spiritual without becoming weird? That will be the theme of another chapter, but let me suggest four things at this point. Number one is to be consistent with your devotional life. In the process of this, you should constantly check things with the Word of God because not every voice is from God. We are admonished in 1 John 4:1, *"Beloved, do not believe every spirit, but test the spirits to see whether they are from God"* (NAS95). Check all voices with the authority of God's Word, and let all voices be submitted to that authority. Then I need to be open to and submitted to others in the Body of Christ. Ephesians 5:21 enjoins us to *"submit one to another."* Hebrews 13:17 charges us to *"obey them that have the rule over you, and submit yourselves: for they watch for your souls."* The Old Testament passage in Proverbs 11:14 reminds us, *"Where no counsel is, the people fall: but in the multitude of counselors there is safety."* I am not hesitant, even during revival type services to check in with other mature leaders to see if they have a witness to the leading I sense in my spirit. Sometimes a holy huddle by members of the five-fold ministries (Ephesians 4:11) is exactly what is needed.

A third preventive to spiritual weirdness is to be well rounded. Before you were born again, you were born. The reality is that God created the whole you and He is delighted with what He made. In intense moves of God, we have learned that you need to take some breaks, to do some things that may not appear overtly spiritual. Do some family things. Learn to laugh at yourself, because everyone else is already doing this. Sometimes the most spiritual thing I can do is to play a round of golf or teach a worm how to swim (go fishing).

My wife once counseled one very zealous lady to stay home from a revival service and seduce her unsaved spouse who was becoming quite suspicious of where his wife was going night after night.

Beware of the Deadly D's

During the days of the Brownsville Revival Pastor John Kilpatrick taught us to beware of the deadly d's. The first of those is doubt. Do not be surprised when the devil tries to cause you to doubt the validity of your experience in Jesus. Perhaps we need to doubt our doubts a bit more. If Satan can get you to doubt the reality of what Jesus has done in your life through revival, he can take you out of the revival.

The second of the deadly d's is distraction. The devil will try and distract you from following after God with all your heart. I have watched both pastors and parishioners simply get distracted, lose their focus and the desire for revival slips away. This can happen to good people.

The deadly "d" for others is disappointment. We are encouraged in Hebrews 10:35-36 to *"cast not away, therefore, your confidence, which hath great recompense of reward. For ye have need of patience, that, after ye have done the will of God, ye might receive the promise."* (KJV) Even in revival, you will face disappointment. Not every service blows the top off the roof. Preachers will fall off their pedestal. Your expectations will not always be met.

The next deadly "d" is closely related to disappointment. It is discouragement. Disappointment can give way to discouragement. Perhaps the person you hoped to see saved did not respond. You feel like everyone else in the church has a great story except you. Overwhelming discouragement can cause you to give up. I love the gift of prophecy, but sometimes a long series of unfulfilled prophecies bring discouragement. You feel like the carrot is always dangling just beyond the reach of the donkey. You feel the bright light in the tunnel is an approaching express train positioned to run you over. During the early days of the Outpouring in Terre Haute, Indiana, a preacher expressed to me he was experiencing the challenge of discouragement. In previous moments they had felt they were on the edge of revival, but in every instance that hope had been dashed, and he was almost afraid to hope again. Discouragement was a snare he had to overcome.

Defamation is the final deadly "d" to consider. While it is true leaders are not immune to falling into sin, it is also true Satan specializes in false accusation. He will try to tarnish the reputation of the leaders of a revival because he knows if he succeeds, it can stop a revival in its tracks. This is why scripture admonishes not to receive accusations against leadership without two or three witnesses. This was brought home to me during a seven-week revival in Wisconsin. I walked into the pastor's office to be told I seemed to be doing quite well for someone who was in the intensive care unit at the hospital fighting for his life! The pastor had received a phone call from a concerned church member who had heard about my dire situation. They were calling to confirm the diagnosis. As we began to track down the series of events that falsely placed me in the intensive care ward we learned the following. Someone had seen my wife and I out walking that morning. We normally walk around four miles daily. A couple of phone calls later "walking" became the "walk-in" medical clinic. Another couple of phone calls and I had walked into the hospital where I was admitted. This soon became the intensive care unit where I was fighting for my life. Now, I appreciated those who were interceding for my healing, but I actually felt quite fine. I can laugh at that incident, but tragically the same pattern of misunderstood statements can bring great damage to a person's reputation. A wise person once said, "Believe nothing that you hear and only half of what you see."

Let's stoke the flames of revival, not choke them out! Keep the wood on the fire and guard against those things that smother flames.

6

LIVING OUTSIDE OUR COMFORT ZONE

"But as his anointing teaches you about all things" – 1 Jn 2:27
"Search the scriptures;" - Jn 5:39

Living in revival is one of the greatest privileges a person can have given to them. It can also be one of the most challenging things a person can ever face. I believe pastoring a revival is God's goal for every pastor, but it can also be an incredibly challenging thing. I sat with a denominational executive during the revival of the 1990s who told me he was receiving the most incredible stories of his nearly 30 years in his office. Churches were experiencing the greatest moves of God they had ever known. It was wonderful! However, not every phone call brought reports of glory. Some pastors described the whitewater ride of revival to be a bit more than they had bargained for.

In the little book by James Burns that I mentioned in a previous chapter, he outlined not only the conditions preceding revival but also the events that follow revival. Two of those events were phenomena and opposition.

It seems God refuses to live inside the boxes we construct for

Him. Every church has a box. Every church has an ethos and a code of conduct they expect God to maintain. I do not mean to insult anyone with the following illustration, but if you bear with me, I believe you will understand the point I am trying to make. When God goes to what is called a "high church" He is expected to behave in a particular manner. The outline of the service is usually placed in our corporate hands. We know when to stand...to sit...to pray...to repeat...to listen. I was praying with a pastor from such a church who suddenly cried out, "Oh, God please do something that is not in the bulletin."

If I leave this type of church and go to what is considered a more mainline or evangelical church, I may discover a bit more informality. The air may be punctuated with more "amens," and the clapping of hands during the singing of songs is more accepted than in the high church. However, there are still guidelines. The meeting is certainly led from the front. God is expected to refrain from placing a prophetic word in the heart of a worshipper. And by all means, He should never prompt someone to pray aloud in tongues.

If we go down the street to the Pentecostal or Charismatic church, we may notice it is more "freewheeling." Lifting of the hands as they worship is likely to be more common. An utterance in tongues does not strike great uncertainty into the heart of those familiar with pentecostal worship norms. God is permitted to do that, but there will still be restraints on what is acceptable and what is not. Still, some things are met with resistance. Let me illustrate.

A Bible College president of my acquaintance was speaking to a nationwide gathering of the state leaders of his group. In his message, he addressed the comfort zones or ways we expect God to conduct Himself in our churches. When he spoke of clapping hands and lifting holy hands before the Lord the leaders were with him. But then he suggested they practice another Biblical expression of worship. He suggested they dance before the Lord, observing that the Bible contained more references to that expression than to clapping, after which he had them all stand and position themselves far enough apart, so they could dance. They were quite relieved when instead of insisting on the dance he allowed them to return to their seats. All recognized dancing was in the Bible, but it was not within their comfort zones. Some were prepared to stretch themselves, while others suggested he was a wise man who knew when it was time to stop.

What do you do when revival moves outside the box? What do you do when God appears to be interested in stretching your comfort zones?

In the revival of the last decade of the 20th-century pastors indicated to me their shock at the discovery of comfort zones they had not known existed. Some were comfort zones within their congregations. Some were comfort zones within their hearts. More than one pastor told me he was stunned at those in his church who rejected revival when it came. They had been praying for many years for God to send revival, but when it came, God did not package it the way He had packaged previous moves. Because it was outside of their box some simply could not accept it. They had an image of what revival needed to look like and when the present one did not conform they convinced themselves this could not be God.

Often the struggle over revival has been with phenomena such as people falling on the floor or shaking. Sometimes it has been the occurrence of dreams or visions. At other times the issue has been the intrusion of the gifts of the Spirit or healing miracles breaking into the flow of the meeting. Perhaps less dramatic, but often more problematic, has been the introduction of different expressions of worship.

So, what are you to do when God appears to be operating outside of the box? Does revival require us to embrace every new and strange thing as coming straight from the throne of God? Should we set up "revival police" who investigate and evaluate everything to determine whether we embrace it or reject it?

Let me begin by simply observing revival will probably stretch you! God will occasionally go outside of your box. As for me personally, He seems to have enjoyed destroying boxes that I had created for Him. Revival will take you there.

Two extremes must be noted. Some will embrace everything that comes along during a revival. Others will reject everything that is new to them. Some will not only go "where no man has ever gone," but they will also go where no angel has ever been or intends to go! Others will be so entrenched in their position that no amount of dynamite will move them.

Those pastors who are reading this book will probably have three desires. You want to please God. You want to see your church grow and thereby see the Kingdom grow. You want to see your people ministered to. So, what are the principles to consider as a spiritual leader? I want to consider five safeguards when deciding if this is God stepping you outside your comfort zone. Then I want to consider three ways to avoid being trapped by the counterfeit.

Can You Show Me That in Scripture?

We were ministering in what became a six-week revival in a church in the eastern part of the United States. I had received a phone call just minutes before the service from our personal intercessors, and this caused me to be a bit late entering the auditorium. As I stepped through the door, the entire church was standing on their feet clapping. No one was at the podium, and they did not appear to be responding to human direction. I found my place and began to join them. It soon became apparent they were clapping unto the Lord. After several minutes of the sustained clapping, I asked the Lord what was going on. In my spirit, I heard Him say this is a Psalm 47 service, so I opened my Bible to that portion of Scripture. The opening line in the KJV says, *"O clap your hands, all ye people."* The next line reads, *"shout unto God with the voice of triumph."* Just as I was reading this phrase, the congregation broke into spontaneous shouts of worship to the Lord. Thinking to myself this is interesting I continued to read the Psalm. Verse three says, *"He shall subdue the people under us, and the nations under our feet."* As I was reading that line, the entire congregation broke into dancing or jumping before the Lord. Verse five begins with *"God is gone up with a shout."* Sure enough, after a few minutes of exuberant dancing, the congregation again lifted the rafters with shouts. By now I was fully engaged with the chapter.

The next line in verse five reads, *"the Lord with the sound of a trumpet."* I said to the Lord, "I've got you there because I am the only trumpet player in this auditorium, and I do not have my trumpet with me." Just as I was saying this to the Lord the man on the keyboard, whom I had judged as being fairly carnal, pushed a few buttons on the keyboard and began to only play one key at a time. And yes, you guessed it. The sound coming from the keyboard was that of a trumpet! I turned to the pastor, who was standing next to me, and told him "I know what is going to happen next." I showed him the flow of the Scripture, and he saw how it related to the pattern of the service. I said the next thing that should happen according to verse six is singing because that verse reads *"Sing praises to God, sing praises: sing praises unto our King, sing praises."* As we were looking at the verse the entire congregation, roughly 135 that morning, broke into the same song. Now all of this happened with no one standing at the podium giving directions to the meeting. It was a morning where it appeared God did church the way He wanted to do it.

The purpose of telling this story is to emphasize the role of Scripture. When the service took on a flow that was not the normal pattern, God took me to a passage of Scripture that explained what He was doing at that moment. Revival will have these moments that are not ordinary. In those moments there will be a balance and support between Scripture and Spirit. Normally, the Scripture, which is the foundation of all we do, will support or explain the activity of the Spirit. The Spirit will never give direction contrary to the Scripture. However, there are times when the Spirit will give a better understanding of what is in the Scriptures. Here is an example.

The prophet Joel had been read many times before the Day of Pentecost, but on that day the Holy Spirit gave Peter a fresh understanding of God's Word. The passage had always been there. Religious leaders had probably spoken from the passage or at least discussed and debated it, but on that day the Spirit gave Peter an application beyond what any could have dreamed. It was not a teaching contrary to God's Word, but it gave an understanding that had not been grasped before. Not only did the apostles make constant reference to Old Testament passages and then showed how they were fulfilled in Jesus (Acts 3:22-23; 4:25-26; 8:30-35 [Philip the evangelist]; 13:32-42) but it was also the combination of the Spirit acting with or on the Word that gave them understanding as to what they were to do. In Acts 13:45 the Jews rejected the message preached by Paul and Barnabas, so they turned to the Gentiles and proclaimed God's good news to them. This turning to the Gentiles was based not only on the rejection by the Jews but in Acts 13:47 by a revelation or understanding of Isaiah 49:6.

This same pattern is seen in the gathering of the church leaders in Acts 15 where they came together to evaluate this expansion into the Gentile world. The revelation by the Spirit to Peter on the rooftop in Acts 10 which had sent him to the house of Cornelius, now supported by the *"miracles and wonders God had wrought among the Gentiles"* (Acts 15:12) through Paul and Barnabas, followed by a new understanding by James in Acts 15:15-18 of Amos 9:11-12, led to the embracing of the Gentiles as brothers in Christ. The Spirit gave them a proper understanding or application of God's Word. Indeed, one could argue much of the writings of the Apostle Paul are a revelation by the Spirit of Old Testament principles that had only been partially understood. I am not proposing an open canon, but I am saying during seasons of revival the Holy Spirit will often give an application from a passage of Scripture to a situation. Let me say again that I believe the Scripture is our final plumb line. However, sometimes the Spirit explains the Scripture without violating the bounds of proper Biblical exegesis. At other times the

Scripture explains the activity of the Spirit.

Does it Violate Scripture?

Perhaps another way to explain this concept is to ask, "Does this impression or apparent activity of the Spirit violate Scripture? Is there either plain Scripture that indicates this 'activity of the Spirit' is wrong or does this so-called activity of the Spirit violate the principles of Scripture?" When I am evaluating a possible leading of the Spirit during a service, I look for plain Scripture from the Lord. If that is not there, I ask myself does this leading run contrary to the nature of Scripture?

The great apostle John, under the inspiration of the Holy Spirit, closes the gospel bearing his name with these words, *"And there are also many other things which Jesus did, the which, if they should be written every one, I suppose that even the world itself could not contain the books that should be written"* (John 21:25 KJV). Hebrews 2:3-4 (KJV) tells us the message of salvation *"which at first began to be spoken by the Lord, and was confirmed unto us by them that heard him; God also bearing them witness, both with signs and wonders, and with divers miracles, and gifts of the Holy Ghost according to his own will."*

The principle I am trying to explain is the Scripture is not a straitjacket, but we need to be careful here. John says Jesus did many things that were not recorded in Scripture. The writer of Hebrews indicates it was the combination of the spoken message and the signs and wonders which served as confirmation. I do not necessarily need chapter and verse to tell me a particular action is acceptable. However, that action will never violate the spirit of the Scripture.

Let me illustrate. Revival is often preceded by and nurtured by intercession. My wife has led groups of intercessors. She and I together have led scores if not hundreds of prayer meetings over the years. Sometimes an intercessor will be led by the Lord to do a "prophetic act," or a "Spirit-led illustration." During a prayer meeting which occurred in a fifteen-week revival, I was strongly impressed there would be people in the meetings that week who were in bondage to sin. I had a sense it was like they were trapped behind a gate or fence and that we needed to open the gate, so they could be released to come to the altar. I asked the prayer warriors to stand at the end of each row of seats and in the Name of Jesus to open an invisible gate and allow the sinners to come through the gate to the altar. My mind and spirit were drawn to Isaiah 45:1-3 (KJV), *"Thus saith the Lord to his anointed, to Cyrus, whose right hand I have holden, to subdue nations before him; and I will loose the loins of kings, to open before him the two leaved gates; and the gates shall not be shut; I will go before thee, and make the crooked places straight: I will break in pieces the gates of brass, and cut in sunder the bars of iron: And I will give thee the treasures of darkness, and hidden riches of secret places, that thou mayest know that I, the LORD, which call thee by thy name, am the God of Israel."* I understood contextually that this was a word that God was going to use Cyrus to restore the Jewish people from bondage. God was going to go before Cyrus and would favor him with wealth and power. I did not feel it violated the spirit of the passage to ask God to open the gates or to break in pieces those things holding the sinners captive that week and allow them to experience the treasures of His Kingdom. It became a great week of people getting saved.

On the other hand, I am aware people may abuse this application of Scripture. Intimacy can be an important part of intercession. I have been told of some who felt they needed to illustrate God's desire for spiritual intimacy with His people by engaging in sexual activity. Such activity is a clear violation of *"thou shalt not commit adultery"* and is something the Spirit of God would never, and I underscore, never do. I do not care how many angels danced on the head of the pin if what they told you to do is contrary to Scripture. Do not do it!

Does Your Spirit Bear Witness?

Not every thought that crosses my mind comes from God. I have to sort out the source of the thought. Did it come from my own, often very active, mind? Did it come from something someone said to me earlier? Did it come from an evil spirit? Did it come from the Lord?

We are given a wonderful promise in 1 John 2:27, *"As for you, the anointing you received from him remains in you, and you do not need anyone to teach you. But as his anointing teaches you about all things and as that anointing is real, not counterfeit - just as it has taught you, remain in him"* (NIV). We have been given an anointing from Him and that anointing will teach us. Learn to listen to the anointing that is inside you. This anointing is not the same thing as your mind. Proverbs 20:27 describes the spirit of man as the candle of the Lord. There is a quiet voice that will speak to us from deep inside. It is where the Spirit of the Lord lives. Learn to pay attention to that voice. Never violate it.

Sometimes this witness is also buttressed by your personal experience. Let me illustrate what I am saying. During a month-long revival in southern Illinois, I had an encounter with the travailing part of intercession. The pastor had called for a day of fasting and prayer. While we were praying together over the lunch hour, I found myself in a fetal position in a side aisle weeping. I felt such a strong internal pain and burden for souls. I do not remember how long I wept, but I did so until the burden lifted. It did that, just as suddenly as it had come. The following Sunday saw the greatest response to salvation during the entirety of that month. That burden never came on me in quite the same way again. However, my wife began to experience this type of a spirit of travail. My personal experience and witness assured me and her she was not losing her mind.

A number of years ago we were on the final night of meetings in the state of Arkansas. The altar service was winding down, and I was sitting on the floor at the rear of the platform or stage area. I had decided to go to the pulpit and close the meeting when a man at the rear of the auditorium began to drone in tongues. After listening a few moments, I decided to shut him down and close the meeting. Immediately a very strong sense came into my spirit not to do so. I felt very strongly I was not to touch what was happening. At least twice I started to get to my feet to stop thc droning, and both times the same very strong witness came into my spirit. About this time the sixteen-year-old son of the pastor came to me. He felt God had given him a word to say (perhaps an interpretation). Once again, that very strong inner witness indicated I should give him the microphone, so I did. I do not recall what he said, but as he was speaking people began to return to the altars. Much weeping broke out. Ultimately the one-week meeting became a two-week meeting and possibly a precursor to a later very strong move of God that church experienced. Had I listened to my mind instead of my spirit I would have silenced the droner, and we would have missed what God wanted to do.

What is the Fruit?

Connected to the witness of the Holy Spirit with your spirit is a very simple truth. When God is in something, it will bear fruit. A bit of trial and error may occur here as we learn to listen to the voice of the Spirit speaking to our spirit, but the ultimate test of an impression or a manifestation is found in the fruit it produces.

Many struggle with some manifestations that occur in a revival. I wrote a small book entitled, "What Happens During Revival," where I deal in some detail regarding those various manifestations. I would like to take three quotes from the book. I quote David Womack in The Wellsprings of the Pentecostal Movement on p 79. "The emotional pitch of the revival was high, and many physical manifestations were seen. This brought much opposition to the meetings, but the preachers saw in these emotional outbreaks the results of the conviction of sin and effects of the experience of salvation in their hearers."

Another quote comes from the ministry of Lorenzo Dow, a Methodist evangelist. When the manifestation of being slain in the Spirit occurred in his meetings some supposed it was strictly flesh while others thought it was the work of the devil. Dow responded to the latter by saying, "If it be the devil's work, they will use the dialect of hell when they come to." This quote came from James Gilchrist Lawson in <u>Deeper Experiences by Famous Christians</u> on p 163.

During the Brownsville revival at the close of this past century, the leaders of that revival asked themselves five questions regarding manifestations. John Kilpatrick records them on p 99-100 in <u>Feast of Fire</u> which I also quoted in my small book.

1)   Is Jesus being lifted up?
2)   Is this creating a greater hunger for God and His Word?
3)   Is this leading people to love God and each other more?
4)   Is this bringing truth and greater spiritual depth?
5)   Is there any practical change taking place (sometimes this must be judged over time)?

In other words, Pastor Kilpatrick was asking, what is the fruit? According to Jesus in Matthew 7:15-20 the fruit tells us the source. Fruit is not "Do I like it?" Rather, it includes the list above. Are they falling more in love with Jesus? Are they becoming more like Him? Has their hunger for Him increased as a result?

One of the more unusual services I ever experienced occurred while I was serving as a pastor. We were in a series of meetings with an evangelist and guest musicians. At one point the evangelist left his seat next to me, ran to the front of the stage, grabbed the hand of the lead female singer and began skipping around the auditorium. While I sat there thinking *"That's strange"* two of my more conservative deacons left their seats in the auditorium to run to the stage, take the hands of two more members of the team and join in the skipping. I suddenly found myself with a very strong urge to join them, and so I jumped up grasped the hand of a male singer and pursued the other three couples. I think we skipped around the auditorium twice. Seven of the eight skippers were rejoicing in the Lord. One was praying the media would not enter our auditorium. That would have been me. We finished skipping by standing at the altar worshipping. Nobody else budged. At the close of the service, the leaders of that group sat down with me to share what was happening from their perspective. The group was composed of seven members. Four of the seven were even then facing the deepest crisis of their ministry. Would you like to venture a guess on which four? I cannot explain why or how it worked, but somewhere in that skipping God broke through into their lives, and what could have destroyed them did not do so. Now, I am not telling you this to announce a new skipping doctrine. In fact, I have never done that since, although I will if so instructed by the Lord. The point is simply that the fruit of the unusual manifestation verified it was from the Lord. I have learned to be slower to pronounce *"Ichabod"* over something I do not understand, but give it time to see if God is indeed in it.

What Do Others Think?

God has given us several ways to determine if an action is His or not. If there is no clear indication from Scripture, if your sense is not clear either, God has given you the body of Christ. What is the witness of others you trust?

Not everyone who speaks to a situation should. Not long ago a revival broke open at a church in New Zealand. I was asked by someone not connected to that revival if I would be willing to speak into it. My response was it would be inappropriate for me to speak into what I had not been invited to speak into. However, if the leader of that revival was interested in my input, I would be willing to talk with him. I am amazed or amused at the people who are willing to speak into situations they know nothing about. A friend in the States who saw a significant revival come to his church told me he received numerous phone calls with counsel he had not sought. He told me he received phone calls suggesting the revival be moved from his place to their place for various reasons. Sometimes you have to protect yourself from what others are saying.

Having said that, the Scripture still teaches safety can be found in a multitude of counselors (Proverbs 11:14). I am not so egotistical as to think I am the only one who can hear from God. How does that work out in a revival type of service? I may have an impression, but I am not in charge of the meeting. I either wait until the meeting is given to me to proceed with what I sense, or I take the leader aside and share what I am sensing and ask how that sits with what he or she is sensing? If it is the Spirit, agreement will come. If the agreement is not there, I do not go any further with it. Sometimes the service is in my hands, but I have some question about what I feel we should do. I will either talk to the leader of the meeting, who is usually the pastor of the church, or I may converse with my wife.

Since August of 2010, I have been connected to an Outpouring taking place in the state of Indiana. I began as the lead evangelist. Other voices now speak into the Outpouring, but I suppose I am still considered a key voice. From early days we would convene a holy huddle on the stage or the front row depending where we were sitting. The huddle would often consist of the pastor, who is apostolic, a recognized prophet, and myself. A visiting missionary spoke to me of the safety she felt watching us in the huddle. We were checking out what we sensed with each other. Often the prophets in that Outpouring are quick to run prophetic words past me before they share them in public.

When God began speaking prophetic-type words to my wife for a meeting, she would first come to me and share what she felt. She was prepared to submit her sense to my wisdom. She still does that. In the early days, I would often share a direction for the service she had felt without identifying her as the source. Now, I am more likely to hand her the microphone.

I am not afraid to confirm the leading I have with those I trust.

What About the Counterfeits?

Some are so afraid of the counterfeit they refuse to embrace the genuine. Yes, there are false prophets. Yes, there are overly enthusiastic people who will miss God. No, you are not perfect, and you will make mistakes from time to time. Relax, God is not about to fall off His throne.

You do not deal with counterfeit cash by throwing out the good stuff. Bank tellers are taught to recognize the counterfeit by handling the authentic. The more you are exposed to authentic moves of God, the more rapidly you will recognize both that which is genuine and that which is not. Hang out with revival leaders. Attend services where it is happening! Watch how the leaders deal with situations. I practiced this during the Brownsville revival. I went to receive from the Lord, but I also went to learn. I watched Steve Hill preach and give altar calls. I watched John Kilpatrick give oversight to the meeting. I spent time with Carey Robertson, the senior associate. In fact, I developed a hot line to Carey's desk!

We had a preacher who was powerfully impacted by the Outpouring in Terre Haute. Later, he became the evangelist at a six-month revival. He told me when confronted with situations in the service where he did not know what to do he would ask himself, "What have I seen Michael do in these situations?" Learn from the authentic, and you will not often be caught up by that which is not.

To avoid the counterfeit, spend a great deal of time in the Word of God. Live in it! This means more than knowing a few random verses. The more you spend time in the Word the more you will come to understand the nature of God and how He operates. You will not only come to know chapter and verse, but you will also come to know the spirit of the words.

A lady who was upset with people falling to the ground during a meeting I was preaching challenged it by saying to me, "My God does not do that." But the reality is that the God of the Bible did do that. I can take her to 20 some passages of Scripture where He did. I could take her to the pages of history to show her He did "do that." The question was not "Does God do this?" but rather was this particular moment from God?

My final suggestion for dealing with the counterfeit is to spend much time praying in the Spirit. You will come to recognize Him. Jesus told a group of religious leaders they were in error because they did not know the word nor the power of God. Mt 22:29 (KJV) *"Jesus answered and said unto them, Ye do err, not knowing the scriptures, nor the power of God."* We need to know the Scripture, but we also need to know the power of God. Many are powerful in the Word, but they are still weak in the power or the Spirit. It is both spirit and truth. In His conversation with the Samaritan woman, Jesus stressed this combination (John 4:23-24). It takes two wings for a bird to fly.

The more you pray in the Spirit, the more you will come to know Him. Did you ever receive a phone call, before the days of caller ID, where the voice on the other end asked the question "Do you know who this is?" You stalled as long as you could. You tried to come up with a name but finally had to admit you did not know your caller. Once they identified themselves, you knew them. Why did you not know them before? Because it was not a voice you heard frequently. My wife never identifies herself to me on the phone. She just begins, "Hey, honey." There are many people called honey, but I know immediately who she is. Why? Because I spend a lot of time with her. I know her voice!

Some years ago, my secretary was told I believed a certain thing. She responded by saying to the person "I will categorically deny he said that or believes that." She went on to say, "I know him, and I know he does not think that way." Now, I have no idea what I was supposed to have believed or spoken, but one who knew me knew it was not so. I encourage you to spend much time praying in the Spirit and hanging out with Him. You will come to know how He thinks, feels, and acts. The counterfeit will not impress you.

7

A CASE STUDY: AUSTRALIA AND ALABAMA

Southern Fires

As revival broke open in our lives and ministry my wife and I determined to be students of revival. We not only added a number of books to our personal library, but we sat down with leaders whose churches were experiencing some level of revival. Initially, our conversations were of the "Why is this happening in your church?" nature. Later we began asking "How do you sustain revival in your church?" We even asked such pragmatic questions as "How did you know when to bring a series of revival services to a close?"

Shortly after we visited the Brownsville revival, we were preaching meetings in northern Mississippi. We heard about a church in a small town in northern Alabama experiencing a revival, so we drove over for two services on the nights between our own services. I was told by the pastor of that church that in fifteen weeks of revival services 997 people responded to a salvation altar call. Close to 500 were filled with the Holy Spirit. This occurred in a church that averaged roughly 150 on a Sunday morning in a town of about 7,000. On a later drive through that community I was able to spend time with the pastor. When I asked him what, in his opinion, led to this visitation from God he observed two things. First, was the sovereignty of God. A sovereign God can do what He wants…where He wants…how He wants…and to whom He wants. On the human side, he put the revival down to hunger. He had a good friend in ministry who was related to a staff pastor at Brownsville. Before the revival broke at his church, he often accompanied this friend to that revival. Being in that revival increased his faith and hunger for his own church and city. That hunger was expressed by a weekly 48-hour prayer meeting. The prayer meeting would begin on Friday morning and continue straight through until the Sunday morning worship began. This prayer meeting continued for a number of months before the revival exploded.

It was shortly after visiting this revival that our first extended meeting broke open. At one point, I placed a call to the Alabama pastor to ask, "How do you know when an extended meeting is over?" He simply said, "You and the Pastor will know." Certainly, I have been in meetings where the voice of the Holy Spirit was incredibly clear. I am thinking of an instance when the Lord spoke to my heart and told me the Pastor would ask me to extend the meetings, and the answer was to be "No." I did not understand that answer until four weeks later when I walked into the greatest spiritual explosion of my life.

That same Alabama Pastor gave me three things they looked at when the voice of the Spirit was not crystal clear. I have added one more. I have found these guidelines to be very helpful.

First, ask yourself if the crowds are there. If the people are not coming, you can call it anything you want, but it is not revival. This does not mean you will always have increasing crowds. Most extended meetings have at least one night in the week that is a low attendance night. There is an ebb and flow in attendance. Even during revival community events, school activities, and family happenings can all impact the crowd. Ask yourself, "Why is the attendance down?" Do not panic at the first low night. You will probably rebound in attendance. Do not fear that the people will only remember the low nights at the end. Most will only remember the great nights! In cowboy language, "ride the horse" as long as you can. More mistakes are probably made by cutting a meeting off too quickly rather than extending it too long.

The second question I was told to ask myself is, "Do the results merit me asking the next person/church to delay the scheduled ministry?" This addresses the number of salvations, Spirit baptisms, healings and the like. This speaks as well to the changed lives.

Thirdly, "Are the finances there?" God will not bankrupt a church for the sake of a meeting. Neither will He bankrupt the evangelist for the sake of a meeting. He may stretch your faith now and then, but finances may be an indicator of where a meeting is at.

The fourth indicator relates to the manifest Presence of God. "Is He there?" You cannot dictate an awesome Presence of God. The testimony from the Brownsville revival in Pensacola, Florida, was they kept extending the meetings because they were afraid He might not keep coming and they did not want to miss the opportunity to be with Him. Open heavens are often clear indicators to keep the meeting going. Certainly, open heavens are stronger than simple anointing.

One more time I want to emphasize the clear voice of the Spirit must take precedence. Some of the greatest results we have seen have come after we were tempted to shut down an extended meeting, but felt checked in doing so.

Advice from an Aussie

In 2002 I was introduced to an Australian pastor who was seeing revival in his church. He was the guest speaker at a meeting for preachers I had attended just to be refreshed. I was told the revival in his church had run somewhere around four years at the time. Over lunch, I asked him what he felt were the keys to sustaining the move of God. In response to my question, he mentioned four things that seemed to be important.

First, he talked about the sovereignty of God. First Corinthians 13:12 states that we "see through a glass darkly." Sometimes we cannot be certain of the cause of revival. One church prayed for two and a half years and then revival came. Another pursued that same Presence for ten years before the longing of their heart was satisfied. We can and should learn the principles of both attracting and sustaining the Presence of God. At the same time, we recognize a sovereign God may not explain all His thinking before revival comes.

Secondly, he spoke about faith. Many people always believe God for something to be over. He said to me, "Whenever you believe revival is over then it is over." He determined to live in and encourage a positive faith-filled attitude about revival in his church. He always believed this Sunday would exceed last Sunday.

His third principle was the releasing of the prophetic in his church. I told him he had just become a controversial figure for many pastors with that statement. Almost all pastors will agree to the role of God's sovereignty. Many will understand the importance of living by faith. The prophetic, however, can be scary. He indicated he could only speak for himself, but there was something about releasing the prophetic that seemed to sustain the revival for his church. In the years since that conversation, I have observed its basic truth, which should not surprise us because the Scripture points toward the prophetic as being a part of the last days revival.

His final principle was to lay hands on his people regularly. This may not have included every meeting, but they discovered something seemed to stir inside of people when hands were laid on them. The doctrine of laying on of hands was revived for many Pentecostals during the revivals at Toronto and Pensacola. Certainly, this teaching has experienced its share of abuses over the years, yet I would suggest this pastor is accurate. Often, when the evangelist leaves town, the pastor goes back to church as normal. During the special meetings people are prayed for almost nightly, but when those meetings end, often the laying on of hands is one of the first things to go. To be honest, sometimes it is because we preachers do not want to be embarrassed because nobody falls over when we touch them. One candid friend of mine served as an advisor for a charismatic women's ministry. While he is the best I have heard teach people how to share their faith, people rarely fall to the ground when he prays for them. He candidly admitted that his prayer line was usually the shortest when he was asked to pray for people. We must move beyond first impressions. Let's allow our people to be prayed for on a regular basis and stir up what God is doing in them.

Both of the above situations involved churches where I have never preached. I did attend the meetings in Alabama, but I have never been to the church in Australia. However, I have provided you with these two case studies because I have shared their principles with some of the churches where revival broke out, and they found those principles were helpful on their journey.

In the next chapter, I want to present case studies on churches and cities where the longest meetings I have preached occurred. At least three of those churches are still at some level of revival as I write this book.

8

A CASE STUDY: LEVIN, NZ 2008

Revival often seems a mixture between the "suddenlies" of God and the preparation of men. At one level, revival is never planned for but is a spontaneous reaction between heaven and earth. On another level, it is very definitely planned for. It is planned in the heart of God, and it is planned in the heart of man. Planning in the heart of man does not mean every "i" is dotted and every "t" is crossed. Often the planning is more a preparation of the heart than a preparation of the mind.

Levin 2008 was never on my calendar. My 2008 schedule for New Zealand was to take us to Southland where we would spend a month ministering at churches and regional gatherings of pastors from a particular denomination. When we arrived in New Zealand, we discovered the work being done on our apartment in Lower Hutt was not quite finished. We needed to "disappear" for another couple of days until they could finish it up, so we decided to drive about 90 minutes north to Palmerston North and check into a hotel room there. We planned to sleep and allow our bodies to adjust from jet lag. On the return trip, we made an impromptu decision to call in at the home of Tony and Lynette Collis in Levin for a cup of coffee and a catch up. Tony and Lynette had been a part of the 20-week revival in Lower Hutt in 2000 and again the seventeen-week one the following year. During that time frame, Tony was serving as an itinerant evangelist, so we hit it off quite well. His wife had been profoundly impacted by the 2000 meetings; I think life-changing is a good description. A little less than two years earlier, they had been asked to go on staff at the Assemblies of God church in Levin, and roughly three months before our stop for a cup of coffee and conversation Tony had been asked to serve as the senior pastor of this church.

Over the coffee, Tony excitedly shared with us the growing hunger in his church. It had been a good church for many years, and Tony had followed a long-term pastor. However, Tony's predecessor, Ray Perry, was still in the church. He had resigned the pastorate to go to Thailand as a missionary, and while his itineration process was in process, he was still considered a staff pastor with Ray and Tony switching roles. Tony shared with us the stirring happening among his men. Spontaneous prayer meetings were occurring as men would text each other with a desire to get together and pray. While we had coffee, one of those men "happened" by Tony's house. His excitement and hunger were contagious. While we were finishing our coffee and conversation, Tony asked me when our schedule would permit us to come to Levin and preach. I told him our schedule was full for the projected six months we were going to be in New Zealand with only one exception. The only free date was just ten days away. I expressed my reservation that he would not be able to do adequate promotion of meetings with such a limited time frame. He responded that he was rostered to preach that Sunday and felt it was right that we come on that day. Tony suggested we plan for the Sunday morning to be a morning for evangelism. He wanted me to share the Gospel as he had watched me do so many times before. His suggestion for the Sunday night was to make it an emphasis on the Holy Spirit. I love both of those emphases, and so we agreed to go for that.

A Case Study: Levin, NZ 2008

The Sunday morning was a good day of evangelism. Approximately 180 people filled the auditorium for that service. I delivered a straightforward salvation message with six to eight persons, if my memory is accurate, responding to the invitation to give their lives to Christ. Then, Sunday night came! I think the best description is a Holy Ghost explosion happened! I do not recall what I preached, but I do recall a very strong Presence of God at the altar-time (prayer ministry time), and also, Tony being pretty well wasted on the floor. Somewhere around 11 pm, as Linda and I were preparing for the return drive to Lower Hutt, Tony crawled off the floor. His question was, "Can you come back and preach next Friday through Sunday?" My response was "I need to talk to Seth Fawcet," whose church I was to preach at the next Sunday. Seth was still serving as the pastor of the church where we had experienced the two lengthy revivals mentioned earlier.

So, we agreed that I would discuss the situation with Seth, and Tony would talk to his staff and elders. He assured me he could promote further meetings through text blasts, e-mails, and so forth. Seth's response was classic. He said two things to me. First, "In 2000 and 2001 a number of pastors stood back and allowed you to stay with us during those incredible weeks. Can I do any less?" Secondly, he said "I am praying for God to send revival to my nation. If this is a part of that answer, then I want to work with it." Tony's team was also in agreement with doing further meetings.

On the following weekend, things only intensified. Tony asked us if we could come for another weekend. If my memory is correct, that weekend was going to overlap with the annual Raging Fire Conference at Seth's church, a conference in which I had been a part of the speaking team from its inception. Again, Seth agreed to adjust the schedule so that I would speak in the mornings, leaving me free to preach in Levin for four services that weekend. I can recall sitting in the Pastors' and Leaders' Day which always kicks off that conference, hearing a few pastors teasing Seth over losing his speaker to Tony's revival. All of us were full of both expectation and curiosity.

When Tony asked me if we could go still another weekend, I asked him if we could meet with his leadership team to be sure they were on the same page. So, while Linda and I went to a cafe for a cup of coffee Tony met with his team between the Sunday morning and the Sunday evening services. His phone call confirmed they were all in. Linda and I then raced back to his house to meet with the whole team ourselves.

I am going to be very transparent at this point. I knew Tony was very hungry to see revival come to his church, but I needed to know if it was more than him. I wanted to be sure the entire team was on the same page. Revival is glorious, but it also brings an incredible spiritual pressure. Attacks from the adversary intensify in those seasons, and I wanted them to be aware of that fact. Specifically, though, I wanted to know where Ray, Tony's predecessor, stood on this issue because Tony had been the pastor for only a few months, and that man had been the pastor for over a decade that I was aware of, and probably longer than that. If he was not on board, then this revival was going nowhere. In fact, it would be counter-productive. I listened as each member of the team expressed their belief we were in a God moment, and we needed to respond to that moment. Ray made his conviction quite clear; this was a God thing.

The following Sunday both Ray and Paul, Tony's youth pastor, shared with the church that they believed we were in a God moment. Paul described the feeling of being on an escalator going up and increasing in speed. He had no idea where it was going. He was a bit nervous about the prospect, but he knew it was God. Ray clinched it when he said, "Eleven years ago God tried to do this in our midst, but we missed Him. Let's not miss Him this time."

Public meetings ultimately ran for 19 weeks, Friday through Sunday, interspersed with special meetings of intercessors, cell groups, leader's meetings, staff times, and the like.

The type of stories of things that happened fall into nine

categories.

<u>Attendance:</u> Sunday morning attendance during those 19 weeks went from the average of about 180 to a high of 339. It became nearly impossible to find a seat in that auditorium on a Sunday morning.

<u>Salvation:</u> If my figures are accurate something like 225 people responded to a salvation altar call during those weeks. There are so many great stories out of that number. One involved a young lady in the church who was hosting several ladies in her neighborhood for coffee, where she was able to share with her friends what was happening at her church. One of the ladies was more interested than the others, so the girl from the church asked her if she would like to give her life to Jesus. When she said "Yes," the young lady from the church, who was herself a fairly new convert, told her to wait while she found the prayer they were supposed to pray. Apparently, while I led people in a sinner's prayer at the altar, this young lady had written down what I had said. So, she found the piece of paper with the prayer on it and led the lady in praying a prayer where she confessed she had sinned against God, was sorry for that sin, believed Jesus was the Son of God and invited Him into her life. The story gets even more dramatic. The lady praying to receive Christ had been diagnosed as both schizophrenic and psychotic. That means her problems were having problems! A few weeks later, she shyly shared that from the moment she prayed that prayer the voices in her head had gone away! Will you pardon me while I shout "Hallelujah!" and wipe the moisture from my eyes? I am quite serious about that last comment. As I write this story, I am typing on my computer at a McCafe (McDonald's), and the tears are filling my eyes.

<u>Healing:</u> Where do I start on the healing stories? I am thinking of the elderly man who was due to have surgery for a skin cancer, but before the surgery could be performed the cancer had disappeared, and the doctor told him "You have the skin of a baby where this cancer was." Perhaps I should also share the story of the

man who had a ringing in his ears for many, many years. He became aware one night during a revival service that the ringing was gone. I could talk about the bulimic woman who experienced a total healing from bulimia. One of my favorites was the 40-something-year-old man who was healed of a joint condition in his knees. He was so excited over this that he began running wind sprints in his driveway. His knees were great, but the next day he awoke with some pretty sore muscles.

Sanctification: I have often said my favorite stories during revival usually involve life transformation. One young man told his mother, "I like this revival because you are so much easier to live with." Apparently one or both of them were becoming more Christ-like. One man who had struggled with alcoholism for years awakened one morning as the sun was beginning to come through the drawn shades in his bedroom. As he turned to pick up the beer bottle sitting on the night stand, he became aware the light was forming a perfect cross over the bottle! Call it a coincidence if you like, but conviction and deliverance followed. When the pastoral staff arrived at the office that day, he was in the car park waiting for them. One staff pastor told me, "I have never seen the people living at this level of purity."

Restoration of ministry: I would have done all nineteen weeks of ministry for the story I am about to tell. I think it was the second weekend of the extension when my attention was drawn to a middle-aged man sitting in the center of the middle section of the auditorium. The altar service was winding down with some still sitting and soaking. Others were just getting to their feet at the altar, while still others were beginning to drift out the doors. As my attention was drawn to this man I felt as if the Holy Spirit said, "I want you to go tell him I said, 'He is quality.'" It was such an unusual moment that I sat for a moment and pondered it. I had never had the Lord give me such a word before. I quietly got to my feet and slipped back to the row he was sitting in. He was facing in the other direction and speaking to another party as I approached him. I placed my hand on his shoulder, not to pray, but to quietly get his attention. When my hand touched his shoulder, he fell off his chair onto the floor laughing! He was unable to receive further communication that night. It was not until the next night that I was able to quietly deliver the message I felt God had given me for him. As I shared the word he broke into huge sobs which also ended any communication. It was not until later that I heard his story. Some fifteen or so years before he had pastored a church that had experienced a sovereign visitation from God. Every few weeks the manifest Presence of God would invade their premises. No guest speakers had been scheduled, but God began to turn up. They found themselves in the middle of a sovereign move of God. During that season the growth of the church required a larger building to be erected. It became one of the more prominent churches of its denomination. However, activity increases on both sides of the divide during revival. A pedophile got loose in the church. The wife of a couple in whom many hours had been invested abandoned her marriage to run off with her female lover. Strange, inexplicable things began happening at the worksite of the new building. As he described it, "Things began to spiral downward." In hindsight he recognized the "burden of intercession" he thought he was feeling was actually indicative of a nervous breakdown. He described what happened next to him as an affair. He became vulnerable and sin entered in. On his own he went to the leaders of his denomination to confess his failure. He and his wife were committed to each other and to their marriage. Still, they were stood down from the church and placed on a theoretical program of rehabilitation. After two years of cleaning the church toilets it became clear to the couple that no restoration to ministry was planned by those leaders. He had given his library to family members who were in ministry because he was sure he was unqualified to ever serve again. A man, who was convinced he was unqualified, heard God say, "You are quality." Seven weeks later his wife told me, "We have experienced more restoration in seven weeks than in seven years." I watched God restore the gift of prophecy. I discovered he still had in his files all the procedures they had put in place during the revival fifteen years earlier. For a season he was invited to serve on the staff of a church and later led a city-wide prayer meeting. Yes, I would still do the nineteen weeks for what I watched God do in his life. And the tears are filling my eyes again as I write this.

Restoration of families: I mentioned a 40 some-year-old man who experienced physical healing. Even more important was the healing that took place in his family. Earlier in his life, he had been an associate pastor at a church because "I was good with words." However, he realized while he was good with words, those words had not become a reality in his own life, and one night while leading a home group he realized all the members of his group knew God better than he did. He walked out of the door that night never to walk in again. During this season, he met a spiritualist medium on a beach, with whom the backslidden pentecostal preacher had an affair. Eventually, they got married, started a family, and moved to a town not far from Levin. Somehow, he met Tony who invited him to come that first Sunday we preached. During the years he was away from God, this rather grizzled looking man loved the writings of Dietrich Bonhoeffer and Charles Finney. Underneath it all, he was still yearning for the Presence of God. He told me when he walked into the building on that Sunday night he recognized immediately this was the Presence he had been looking for. He could hardly wait for me to shut up, so he could run to the front and get right with God. When he went home and told his wife what had happened, she wept and wept because God had come, and she had missed Him. They were so excited when they got the text announcing the meetings would continue. During the following nineteen weeks, both their children got saved. The son would come to receive prayer, so he could be slain in the Spirit because it felt so good. His wife encountered a deliverance. Wails turned to sobs and then to chuckles and then gales of laughter at the altar. He told me, "My family says I have changed."

A Case Study: Levin, NZ 2008

<u>Restoration of broken hearts:</u> Every revival has stories that are almost missed. In fact, I am convinced some of the most awesome stories never get told because the person on the receiving end is too shy or just does not realize the depth of what God did for them. We almost missed this story, which concerns a lady who lived on the other side of the Tararua mountain ranges from Levin but had a weekend house in the town. I never heard how she heard about the meetings, but somehow, she did and began to attend. Night after night she stood at the altar or perhaps laid on the floor at the altar encountering the manifest Presence of God. None of us were aware that a few months before her daughter had committed suicide to escape an abusive marital relationship. This mother had discovered the dead body of her daughter and the suicide note. She had blamed herself for not intervening in the abusive marriage, but now as she soaked in His Presence His healing of her broken heart began. It was not a suddenly, but weekend after weekend healing came as she lingered in His Presence. Joy began to replace the sorrow. My tears are starting to flow again as I hear her in my mind telling me the story.

<u>Baptism in the Holy Spirit:</u> I love seeing people filled with the Holy Spirit. In this case, it is not so much about a story, but about a comment made by a staff pastor who said, "I have never seen it so easy to see people filled with the Holy Spirit." When revival comes, and people are very open to Him, this happens.

<u>Manifest presence of God:</u> To me, the signature of revival is that manifest Presence of God. It is the unseen but very tangible sense that God is in the room. The river of God in that building became quite pronounced. One night one of the elders arrived at the building in a mixed state between agitation and awe. As his family was approaching the church building, they could see an orange glow in the sky above where the building was sitting. They were in a panic thinking the building was on fire. However, when they arrived no physical fire existed. They went from agitation to awe as they realized God had let them see a manifestation of His glory. On

101

another evening a CPA had to tell what he had experienced the night before. I point out he was a CPA for two reasons. First, he was a businessman and second he had the stereotypical nature of a CPA. He was a nuts and bolts guy. He had the facts and figures. He could dot the "i" and cross the "t." You may know what I mean. But this man never felt anything. He had gotten saved by faith, and he lived that way. However, the night before, while I was preaching, he saw a cloud above the platform. He said it covered the space I was pacing in as I was preaching. This quiet man began to animatedly run back and forth showing where the cloud began and where it ended.

So, when people asked me, "Is the thing in Levin *really* a God thing?" the answer was an unequivocal "Yes." However, it was also fragile, and I will return to this aspect later.

The Story Behind the Stories

Why did God show up in Levin? I do not know all the answers to that question. I do not know what level of prayer went on historically. I do know that God had spoken to an international prophetess as she was traveling through Levin and told her He was going to send revival to that city. She was so thrilled when she later heard what was happening. However, I do see five stories behind the story. I saw five principles at work in that church.

Principle number one was the sovereignty of God. He brought the right pastor to the right town at the right time. Then He had arranged for the right evangelist/revivalist to not only have a right relationship with that pastor but to be in the country at the right time. He even delayed workmen so an apartment was not quite ready in order that the evangelist and that pastor could have the right conversation at the right time.

Principle number two was the hunger expressed in prayer. The church had both structured and spontaneous prayer gatherings. If memory is correct, they had the odd all-night prayer meeting as well as weekly prayer times. However, it seemed to me the real thrust might have been the spontaneous gatherings of men to cry out together to God.

The third principle was probably a huge key. They had a risk-taking leadership. In fact, I think it is safe to say in every significant revival in which I have been a part, a risk-taking pastor was a part of the equation. Tony was so hungry for God that even the whiff of an oily rag of revival was enough for him. He was prepared to take calculated risks to go after God. He also led the way. I recall one night as I was preaching Tony slid out of his seat onto the floor. He attempted to crawl to his feet later to pray for people, but that attempt was unsuccessful. I had a great picture on an old phone of him spread-eagled in an aisle of the church. Late that night several men joined me in loading Tony into his car. Linda drove him to his house while the men and I followed in our cars. We unloaded Tony from the car and carried him to his bedroom where we rather unceremoniously dumped him on his bed, pulled his shoes off, and announced to his wife he was her problem. Seventeen hours later he came to. His passion for the Presence of God, his passion for souls, and his willingness to take a risk were huge. By the way, during the revival they launched a satellite church in a neighboring town, increased missions giving to record levels, did outreaches in neighborhoods and schools and saw the offerings exceed budget by $1,500 per week.

Principle number four is they were willing to make room for God. Remember Ray, the former pastor, had counseled them, "God tried to do this eleven years ago, and we missed him. Let's not miss Him this time." They sought to make room for Him. This is, first of all, an attitude that is crucial. Too many churches and people want God to be satisfied with the leftovers. Leftover time ... leftover energy ... leftover finances. However, this church adjusted their schedule to fit in with God, and they tried to do it with wisdom. They knew they did not have the manpower to handle services every night, but they did have sufficient worship leaders to allow for a rotation on the weekends that would stretch but not exhaust the team. Weekends (Friday through Sunday) did not conflict with getting up for school or going to work for most people, so they committed that time to God. They permitted God to show up at church, even if it meant adjusting the weekly schedule and adjusting the service time frame. Making room for God will always involve time. It also involves leaving your comfort zones. All of us have them. For some leaving the comfort zone meant showing up at church instead of blobbing out in front of the TV after a busy day at work. For others it meant embracing unusual manifestations of the Spirit, such as people falling to the floor, physically shaking, seeing visions, experiencing deeper intercession, and so on. Sometimes to leave the comfort zone is to give God permission to do things within the life of your pastor and church leadership that you cannot totally explain. While not encouraging a "free for all," I am encouraging a default mode of making room for Him. Allow Him time. Trust Him when He begins to stretch your experiences with Him.

The final part of the story behind this story is evangelism and repentance. A passion for the lost will make room for the lost. The overwhelming bulk of the preaching I did was evangelistic. Repentance from sin was called for. No apologies were made for declaring the Word of God. In every service the gospel was shared, the conviction came, sinners responded. Because the people knew the above was going to happen, they were prepared to bring unsaved friends to the meetings. There is something about an altar full of repentant sinners that keeps filling pews with people.

Levin Was Still Fragile

We finished the nineteen weeks of public meetings with a week of private meetings with staff, elders, cell group leaders, intercessors and other workers. The purpose of those meetings was to discuss how to move from revival type services to a more normal church schedule and keep the flow of revival. I loved the idea. I have been in churches where that transition was done quite well. I think a great effort was made in Levin.

I would like to leave the story right there, but I live in a real world. I should probably insert this disclaimer. The material in all the case studies in this book is from my perspective. Some of the stories could be considered raw. I do not share them to be controversial nor to embarrass anyone. I share them with the desire to assist others who are or will be walking through revival.

For several months after those nineteen weeks of revival things went very well. From time to time I would be there to preach. Somewhere in late 2009 or early 2010, I got an unexpected voice mail from Tony saying, "Hey bud, I resigned the church today." When his wife answered my immediate return phone call in response to my question she said: "2008 was the year from heaven and 2009 was the year from hell." Not everybody had bought into the revival; the annual church business meeting had turned ugly. After reflection, prayer, and consultation with his staff, Tony stepped down.

I knew there had been resistance to the revival. From about week six I knew some had said "no" to revival and "yes" to the religious spirit. However, as long as the church was exploding with growth they stayed below the surface. I think it is fair to observe the following.

Some resented "losing their church." They were comfortable in a religious pattern and did not want to be challenged. We even discovered that while the church was looking at buying property for a new building a man attending the church was bidding against the church for the same property. Others wanted a nice safe, predictable service.

Still, others were not comfortable with the changes in their pastor. They wanted him to have coffee with them. Be safe. Be pastoral. The constant stretching of the church was more than they wanted. It was not that they wanted the pastor to leave, but they did want him to scale back.

For some, it was simply a rerun of the same power struggle

that had been a part of this church for many years. Good people were caught up in the crossfire. Some never understood what was going on. Eventually, more than 50 left the church to go to another one that appeared to be embracing what God was doing.

One couple, who had moved into the town after the revival, asked the pastor if those leading the negative campaign had been a part of the revival. It was probably not until then that they realized that group had come on Sunday mornings but had never allowed the revival to enter them.

A Closing Note

It is possible, and it is my prayer, that Satan overplayed his hand. After two years of itinerant work and personal healing, Tony began a church for those who had never been able to find a place where they belonged. Their hunger for revival would not settle for less. Prayer has become a major focus of that new work.

A second group left the church and during those two years began worshipping at another smaller church. That denomination had sent in a pastor to what was a struggling work. He seems to have had the gifting needed for the moment. That church has gone from a handful to an attendance of nearly 150.

Meanwhile, the former youth pastor became the pastor of the Levin Assemblies of God church. It appears he has been able to stabilize the situation. The church may not be in a wide-open revival, but it is solid. It is probably running around the 180 mark again.

Just recently I heard of another small church in Levin where the hunger is increasing. It may be the devil will end up, not with one, but with three or four on fire revival churches in the town.

Whether that happens or not, I know two things. God will build His Kingdom, and there were people in Levin who will never be the same.

9

A Case Study: Hutt Valley
A Sustainable Journey

I have alluded to the fact I have been privileged to connect with some significant revivals during my life and ministry. One of the great revivals is the one in Hope Centre, Lower Hutt, New Zealand. I have called this case study "A Sustainable Journey" because both the church that hosted the meetings I will allude to and the larger valley have sustained a move of God longer than any other place with which I am personally acquainted.

When introducing Seth Fawcet, the pastor of Hope Centre, John Arnott, who served as the pastor during the great Outpouring in Toronto, observed he knew of only four or five churches that had been able to sustain revival, and Seth pastored one of those churches.

Carey Robertson, who served as the senior associate pastor of the great Brownsville Assembly of God, told me personally he thought it was possible this church in the Hutt Valley might be able to accomplish what they were not able to do in Pensacola.

I first became acquainted with this congregation in 1999. My wife and I had gone to New Zealand to attend the inaugural gathering of a discipleship and deliverance ministry that was being introduced to the leadership of New Zealand. While I was at that meeting, someone pointed Seth Fawcet out to me and suggested I needed to meet him, So, during the next coffee/tea break I wandered over to the tall, bald, happy man (as he likes to call himself) to see why I needed to meet him. This brief meeting and an introduction of my wife and I by Carey Robertson to that conference sparked a word from the Lord to Seth that he should invite us to preach a combined meeting to be hosted at his church. During that weekend, around 45 people committed their lives to Jesus and Seth invited me to return to preach for him in the year 2000. That planned four-day meeting became a 20-week revival, where 800 people surrendered their lives to Jesus, and at least 150 were filled with the Holy Spirit. The outflow of that meeting was an invitation from the pastors of the Hutt Valley (PIM or Partners in Ministry) to return in 2001 and preach a round robin meeting hosted by five churches. That turned into seventeen weeks of services five nights a week where another 750 responded to a salvation invitation. On Sunday mornings I preached not only in those churches but a number of other churches in the city as well. In a period of two or three years, I think I spoke at 20-25 churches in the Wellington region. I have ministered in over 35 now.

In 2010, one of the pastors indicated to me that the blessing the Hutt Valley was living in, which included an estimated increase in church attendance of the valley from 15% to 26%, found its launching pad in those two years. He indicated many of the pastors had had their vision greatly enlarged during that time. Between 2000 and 2010 something like eight different churches had building expansion requests before the city council.

I am grateful to God for the part I was allowed to play in what God did and is still doing, in that church and valley. I remember saying to Seth Fawcet at the close of the 2000 meetings, "I have seen revival break in many churches only to have them drop the ball after we left. Do not drop the ball." At the close of 2001, I told him, "I think this valley could be on the path of transformation. Do not let that train get derailed. That will be harder because it is not just one church you are trying to influence."

When we returned in 2001 to preach what became the 17 weeks of round robin ministry, it was obvious to me the ball had not been dropped. I need to make it clear, the move of God at what was then called Hutt Christian Covenant Centre preceded my ministry at that church. The revival there began in March 1995. The meetings in 1999, 2000, and 2001 simply added a lot of fuel to the fire that was already burning. In 1995 that church probably numbered only around 130. In 1997 Seth and Debbie Fawcet spent eight days at the Pensacola Revival which added to the initial fire. As of this writing closer to 750-800 people call the church home. It has relocated, changed names, and become one of the leading churches not only of the city but the entire region and nation. Its pastoral staff and those sent out from the church have ministered around the world. Its senior leader, Seth Fawcet, not only speaks into revival in New Zealand, but he has had a significant role in what is developing in Europe - Germany, Ukraine, Czech Republic, England, Scotland, and in Asia -India, Sri Lanka, the Philippines. His associate pastor, Graham Renouf, has had a very significant voice into the Outpourings in Indiana and beyond. Other staff and persons sent out by the church have ministered in Vietnam, the Philippines, India, and the islands of the south Pacific. As I have reflected on the revival at that church, I see eight factors at work.

First is the sovereignty of God. I do not say that out of obligation; I say that out of conviction. As I came to know their journey and my journey, it was obvious the sovereign God had stepped in. Let us always acknowledge God is more interested in revival than we are. He is always working and looking for those He can work with.

Factor number two is the role of prayer. The foundation of the revival was a fifty-year 24/7 prayer meeting. For those who thought that was a typo let me make this clear. For 24 hours per day 7 days a week for a period of 50 years, someone in the church was praying.

Most of the time that prayer took place in the prayer room at the church. The background of that prayer meeting was World War II. During the 1940 bombing of London by the German Luftwaffe, the King of England sent out an urgent request for prayer across the British Empire. This request became a mandate for the pastor and subsequently for the church. To be sure not every prayer session was inspired. My wife has conducted interviews with some of the folks who were a part of that season, who will freely admit that some of the time it was boring. In fact, much of the time they prayed out of duty. When the war ended the prayer continued; it became one of the primary reasons the church existed.

At the close of those 50 years, God answered their prayer in a way that the pastor who launched those meetings probably could not have imagined. The founding pastor, Frank Wilson, probably carried an apostolic anointing, and signs and wonders had been a significant part of the early days of the church in the 1930s. They had a room where they kept the crutches and wheelchairs that were no longer needed by people who had been healed. (During the 2000 meetings those wheelchairs were put back into use, but instead of bringing people to church in them people began to be taken out of the church in them.)

One of the significant things God began to do was to bring them out of isolationism. In his book, "Pentecost at the Ends of the Earth" which is a history of the New Zealand Assemblies of God from 1927 to 2003 Ian Clark observes on p. 57 that in the mid-1930s the Commonwealth Covenant Churches (later called the Christian Covenant Churches) came on the New Zealand scene. Their distinguishing doctrine was called British Israelism, which taught that the lost ten tribes of old Israel were now represented by Great Britain, the United States, and the Scandinavian countries. Clark says the best known of those churches was the one located in Lower Hutt. I have heard attendance figures in the range of 600 in earlier times, which would have made it one of the larger churches in the nation 70 years ago. Even before the plea from the King of England, even prior to the bombing of London, the pastor of the Lower Hutt church was given a revelation by God of the bombing that was coming, and he began to publicly preach it was going to happen. Unfortunately, that message was misunderstood by many to be disloyal to the government in a time of war. In fact, it was almost seen as treachery. As a result, the church was persecuted. Apparently rotten tomatoes were thrown at its properties. Other accusations were made as well. Frank Wilson was never married, and certain false allegations were made against him, which also served to damage the church. So, for many years it turned inward and isolated itself from the rest of the Christian community. Legalism was rampant in the church, and holiness was measured by certain external standards. In many places, the church was considered either a cult or at least cultish. Even Seth's wife has candidly observed there was a time the church fit that description. Still, they prayed.

There were three main focuses of the church's prayer during those years; healing, mission, and God to move by His Spirit. You cannot invite God to come to your church and to your valley for fifty years 24/7 without getting heaven's attention. God's answer began to come with the leadership of a new generation. After a decreasing attendance for more than a quarter of a century God raised up its current leadership from within the church. Somewhere a passion for revival was birthed inside of Seth Fawcet, and sporadic moves of the Holy Spirit among the youth group occurred during his leadership. When he became the pastor, he recognized changes had to be made, but he wanted to preserve the prayer DNA. The church was no longer able to carry prayer 24/7, so he dropped that plan, and for the next few years, a 90-120 minute prayer meeting was carried on four times each week. This was functioning during the meetings I preached in 1999-2001. Additionally, every service was preceded by an hour-long prayer meeting. This pre-service prayer meeting still exists, although it is a 30-minute meeting now. When the warriors who had carried the prayer torch for the 24/7 and the 90-

120 minute meeting were no longer able to continue, the plan was changed again. The pastor recognized the old style of prayer was not attractive to a new generation, and an internship was developed for young people. The style changed, but they picked up the baton. Now every two to three months they conduct a week of 24/7, prayer. The youth also host a monthly prayer meeting for the entire church. A dedicated prayer room is a conspicuous part of their facilities. It is on the ground floor of their office complex. The room is constantly updated. In addition to being the location of prayer meetings, it is used for the weekly Healing Room ministry. A smaller group of private intercessors selected by the pastor has also operated. He also sends out a letter to personal intercessors. I want you to notice two things out of this. Prayer has played a large role in the history of this church. Secondly, they have been willing to adapt. The principle is more important than the method. As I write this, the leadership is praying and seeking to find God's wisdom in how to bring the current church into a larger role in prayer. They recognize that many persons who now are part of the church have no connection to the past and its prayer history.

The third factor in the revival at this church is also similar to the one at Levin. That factor is a risk-taking leadership. I sometimes tease the pastor and call him the Phil Mickelson of preachers. Golfers will understand that Phil Mickelson is both an incredibly talented golfer as well as one who is also a great risk taker. Some shots he plays would be attempted by no one else. When he succeeds, as he often does, they are brilliant. Seth Fawcet's approach is to consider what is the best possible thing that could happen and say, "That is worth the risk." Steps of faith have been normal. The church has been on an almost constant building program to accommodate what God is doing. One pastor in the Valley described it to me this way. "We are not surprised that revival would break out at his church first. We often watch Seth go and dive into the river. If he does not drown we follow him in."

But no leader can create or sustain revival by himself. The

church has practiced what I call "followership." The pastor does not struggle to lead the church. The church embraces his leadership and works with him. The people are willing to go where he believes God is leading them. That, my friend, is huge! Many pastors spend as much time fighting their people as they do the devil. Sometimes they are tempted to believe the two are synonymous. It has not always been easy. I am aware of crucial moments in the journey of this church. Early in the pursuit of its revival, there was a group in it that did not want to go there. However, an elderly, retired preacher was used of God to declare the past had been fine. but it was time to adjust. He simply said, "Seth is right, and I am going with him." On another occasion, Seth knew some were not hungry to pursue revival. Some wanted to return to the days of the past. Instead of creating a split he was able to channel the differences into the establishment of a church up in the hills overlooking the valley. Followership made these things happen.

Another key element has been the elders. Seth is a strong leader, but those who share the oversight have sought to avoid dictatorship, which had been a problem in their history. The board of elders has taken national and international revival as a part of the church's assignment. These forward-thinking elders felt "if God wants us to give of ourselves for revival the best we have to give is our pastor." For years they have blessed his international travel as he seeks to take both the fire and the things they have learned in revival to other places. It works because he also has a great staff who can pick up the load with him, a staff that sees their primary purpose is to release him. The elders concur in this.

A sixth element I have noticed is the role of setting the climate in the church building. One of the practical ways they do this is 24/7 worship music in the auditorium. They are not in a position to provide constant live worship there, so the sound system plays 24/7. If a service or an event is not happening, the music is playing. I have stepped into the auditorium to pray when no one was there. I do not think I have ever done so without a sense of God's manifest

113

Presence. Some may prefer to think of this as the lingering of the anointing from Sunday. Call it what you will, but the atmosphere is different because they keep the sounds of worship going in that auditorium. From time to time they receive the stories of repairmen and other visitors wanting to know what they feel in that auditorium.

The seventh element is one of the most important I have observed in Seth. He never gives up on a service! Every pastor reading this book has had one of those services where it is not happening. It is as dry as the Sahara Desert or as frigid as Antarctica. Our temptation at that point is to get the meeting over as fast as we possibly can and hope for better results next time. Seth refuses to give up on a service. He has shared five things he does. First, go with the flow. If there is an obvious thing, the Spirit is doing then go there. Do not swim against the current of the Spirit. If there is no obvious flow, then he is looking for what God is doing in an individual. He calls it "Blessing what God is doing." If he sees someone being moved on by the Spirit of God, he will go and bless what God is doing. He will go to where the action is. Often, he will either go and pray for them or just go and be where they are, which seems to release a similar anointing throughout the building. If no one seems to be the center of the action, then he asks God for a word of knowledge or a gift of healing. He calls it "using the gifting God has given you." Sometimes if the meeting is slow, he will ask God for three words of knowledge and then prays over the person (s) for whom the word came. Others call this stirring up the anointing. If no gift of the Spirit comes, then he may step out in raw obedience to a feeling he has. I can best describe it this way; if it doesn't work, try something else. I have watched him pick up a microphone and change the atmosphere during the worship. He may not have the voice of a concert soloist, but he is not singing a concert. He is prepared to move a service if it isn't moving. A final strategy is the role of the testimony. Sometimes the story of what God has done for someone else will either create faith in others who have a similar need, or it will bring a spark into the service.

The final factor in the Hope Centre revival is the example of its pastors who personally drink from the river of the Holy Spirit and lead by example. They don't watch others worship. They worship. They don't encourage others to enter in. They show them how to do it. It is not unusual for them to be overcome by the Spirit during worship, during preaching, or at other times. Seth often experiences a phenomenon where his legs do not want to hold him up. During these moments strong men often are called upon to help keep him on his feet. He told me once that when this happens, he feels somewhat like a fool. He is a big man. The bottom line for him is this; if being a fool for Christ will encourage others or releases the Spirit he will do it. Sometimes it brings persecution, but he is prepared for that. The spinoff of that is learning how to grasp the three-five-minute teaching moments in the service.

Lest anyone misunderstand me, the church is not perfect, but they have been navigating the white waters of revival for 20 years. Mistakes are made. I have been in meetings where questions were created. The waves may still have troughs, but revival is still their pursuit.

The Valley Itself

As I mentioned earlier in this chapter, from the mid-90s to around 2010 church attendance as measured by attendance at one service per month had risen from 15% of the population of the Valley to about 26%. These figures were given to me by Selwyn Stevens who directs an international ministry based in the Valley. Anecdotal evidence has suggested it may have even been a bit higher. For most pastors and churches these are the good years after many years in the spiritual wilderness. As far back as 2001, I was told that the Hutt Valley was a preacher's graveyard and that I did not understand the type of revival I was a part of.

I have noticed six things which I believe have contributed to this story. First, the key pastors in Lower Hutt have prayed together for many years. Every month they come together to fellowship, worship, pray and prophesy over each other. This is cross denominational, involving Baptists, Presbyterians, and several different Pentecostal or Charismatic streams.

For several years these pastors hosted a monthly city-wide prayer meeting. This was particularly helpful in preparing the city-wide church for the 2001 round robin meetings.

Another prayer connection has been an annual fasting and prayer retreat that brought them together for many years at a retreat center. They usually broke the fast at Burger King, which was rather scary. This shared time cemented both relationships with each other and their mutual burden for the city. In recent years the blessings of revival have presented a new challenge. Growth in the churches and growth in individual ministries have increased the problems in scheduling get-togethers. At least three of the pastors either have or are currently serving on the executive leadership team of their respective denominations. So, for the last three years, the prayer retreat has been shortened to a one-day event.

The pastors believe the role of honor has been very important for what God is doing. They consciously seek to honor each other and to speak well of each other. Two of my favorite Hutt Valley stories come out of this principle. When the pastor of the Assemblies of God church was preparing to attend his national convention, he wanted to take his entire staff and board of elders/deacons to that conference, so he called the pastor of Hope Centre (Seth) and asked if he was willing to pick up any pastoral care needed while the A/G team was out of the city. He instructed his people if they needed pastoral ministry to simply make a phone call to Hope Centre and identify what church they were from and the need would be met. When he told his A/G friends this, they were astonished. They could not believe he was encouraging his people to contact another church. When asked if he could trust that pastor he simply said, "With my life."

The other story involved a relatively large Spirit-filled Baptist and a small Word type of church. The larger Baptist church sent their men over to the smaller church to paint the facility. Worship teams were a strength of the larger Spirit-filled mostly Samoan congregation, whereas worship teams were weak at the smaller church, so the larger church began assisting them. For three weeks each month, the larger church sent a portion of their worship team to assist and train the smaller church, while for one week each month they were on their own so as to not become totally dependent upon those who were teaching them. One Sunday night each month the smaller church closed its evening service and joined the larger church. In that service, the pastor of the smaller church preached.

This honor was seen in 2000 as well. When revival broke out, Seth Fawcet and I determined the revival was for the Valley, not just Seth's church. Response cards were sent to over 50 churches. Pastors began encouraging people to bring unsaved friends to the revival knowing we would send them back. At each altar call discipleship time I encouraged the people to attend church with the friend who had brought them to the meeting. In the 2001 meeting people freely rotated among the churches of the Valley, which had a huge impact on the sense of one church with many congregations or tribes.

Key number five is recognition of the apostolic and other giftings within these pastors. They have no difficulty recognizing and honoring the apostolic and prophetic function some of them have. When Seth leaves the nation to preach it is not unusual for the spiritual leaders to lay hands on him and send him out as their representative.

Finally, I believe the things happening in the Hutt Valley have been made possible because of the longevity of the pastorates. Most of the key leaders have been there over 20 years. They have been doing life together.

Revival, whether in a church or a city, is not static. It is constantly changing. There are crests, and there are troughs in revival. Yesterday's successes do not guarantee tomorrow's success. I harbor a secret fear of taking friends into the Valley lest I find that the fire of revival will have gone out. However, one American pastor put it this way to me. "Michael, I believed your stories because it was you who told them. However, to have twelve lunches or coffees with Pastors from this city and have them all tell me the same story is life-transforming."

Hey guys, let's not derail this train. Let's press in for transformation of our churches and of our cities.

10

A Case Study: Outpouring
in Terre Haute, IN

The challenge that faces me in this chapter is writing a case study of an Outpouring while it is still occurring. This may affect perspective, but I write, as always, from my vantage point.

My wife and I were invited to preach a three-day meeting at Cross Tabernacle in Terre Haute, Indiana, in August of 2010. I had preached a seven-week meeting at that church in 1997, and during that time I had become acquainted with Keith Taylor, a staff evangelist who now serves as the pastor of the church. It was he who invited us to minister at his church.

Cross Tabernacle has long had a reputation for experiencing moves of God. If it is not the oldest Pentecostal church in the Wabash Valley, it is considered the mother church for a number of the Pentecostal churches there. For years it has hosted events where it has invited smaller churches to participate, simply because it has the facilities, people, and passion for doing so. Cross Tabernacle could and would bring in nationally known speakers that other local churches might have found difficult to host. The pastor has long been perceived as a spiritual leader not only in his city but his state as well. He served as a member of the executive leadership of his state's denomination.

On the third day of the scheduled three-day meeting Pastor Taylor asked me if I would be willing to stay one more day, and after the service, on that fourth day, he asked if we could stay one more day again. I remember observing that the depth of the meeting after five days seemed to me to be much greater than after the seven weeks in 1997. On the Friday we flew to Germany to speak at a Conference, Keith took his pastoral staff and drove to Mobile, Alabama to attend the Bay of the Spirit Revival that had broken out there. When Keith walked in the door of that meeting he told the Lord he felt the same type of Presence we had been experiencing in the meetings in Terre Haute. The Lord's response was to tell him there were two differences. The first had to do with the spirit of expectation. The Lord emphasized to Keith that people walked into the Bay of the Spirit with great expectation, but they did not walk into Cross Tabernacle with the same expectation. Secondly, the Lord spoke to him about a strong religious spirit that was dominant in Terre Haute. After this, the Lord indicated that in the third service Keith would know if this was the season he was looking for. Keith rang me in Germany and asked me if we would consider returning to Terre Haute. He made it clear he was not sure that I would preach. He simply wanted me to be in that service because he knew of no one else who had been in as many extended meetings as we had, and he wanted my take on what I felt.

In perhaps one of the greater understatements of my life I rang two pastors, we were scheduled to be with in New Zealand and asked them if they would be willing to release me from my commitment and allow me to re-schedule them at a later time. I remember saying to them, "This is going to sound strange, but I am going to ask you to release me, so I can go sit in a church on a Sunday morning." I went on to say, "I can only say I have this gut-level sense, that if I do not do this, I will regret it."

So, on that Sunday in September of 2010, Linda and I found a place on the front row next to Keith and Karen Taylor. I never left that spot. In retrospect, one did not need a great deal of spiritual insight that morning to realize something significant was happening. On that day, Keith Taylor did the actual preaching. He waited until after the usual dismissal time to call the church to a time of response. I think well over 90% of the congregation rushed to the altar. It was nearly 2:00 pm before the last of the congregation left there. Somewhere around that time, Keith announced services would be held the next night, and these continued for the next two weeks. After this, a church wedding and a state wide denominational event requiring the participation of the pastor obliged us to set meetings aside for one week. The first service after that break was incredibly intense. It was just like we had not taken a break at all.

At that point, we recognized something unusual was taking place. We determined we would not wear out the staff of the church nor the people. For the next month, services were held Wednesday through Friday and Sunday. After that month another adjustment was made. The Wednesday service was returned to the church for a more "normal" schedule. The intent was to provide opportunity for discipleship to happen. Wednesday had long been the night of discipleship emphasis at Cross Tabernacle. In addition to youth ministry, the church was running groups for men and women, boys and girls, and a school of ministry.

Thursday night, Friday night and Sunday night services were held for several months. The emphasis was primarily on "souls." On Sunday mornings, Linda and I began to minister in other churches in the area. The intent was two-fold. First, it was to spread the fire to other churches within a three-hour drive and second to take some financial pressure off the Terre Haute church. After several months of the above schedule, we adjusted that schedule to Friday and Sunday nights.

Every revival we have preached has been different. There are certain things we have learned in all of them. This one has certainly been a journey!

121

A Journey into the Five-Fold Ministries of the Holy Spirit (Ephesians 4:11)

A few weeks into the meetings we were joined by Fred Aguilar. I had known Fred for over 25 years. We had both pastored First Assembly of God in Paris, Illinois. I had preached in his churches. He had also traveled as an evangelist and served as a presbyter of the Assemblies of God for his part of the state of Indiana. When Fred walked into Cross Tabernacle that night, I said to him, "Fred, I have been waiting for you." A few minutes later Keith Taylor said the same thing to him. Fred recognized it was more than him; it was what he represented.

As a boy growing up in Chicago, he attended a church that experienced a three-year revival. Pastors would come from across the nation to the church where they would tell the pastor they had come for a prophetic word. The pastor would say, "I do not have a prophetic word for you, but if you will be in the meeting tonight one of our children will have one." As a ten-year-old boy, Fred was used by God to "read the mail" of these men of God. They began to call him "the little prophet." After that revival closed, due, as Fred told us, to pride which became a huge issue, he went through something of a dark season. Later he was restored to the Kingdom of God, where he served as a pastor, state-wide youth director for his denomination, itinerant preacher and the like. I knew that Fred carried a special anointing, but I did not understand his background.

About 18 months before the Outpouring broke out in Terre Haute Fred underwent surgery. It went so badly that at one point it looked like he would not survive, but two of his "sons in ministry" stopped by his room to tell him they had a word from God for him. He would live and not die; his finest hour was still to come. Then, during the time he was recovering the Lord gave him a vision. He was asking the Lord about some unfulfilled prophetic visions God had given him 50 years earlier, when, in response to his questions, the Holy Spirit said, "I am preparing a man to lead a revival in Indiana and beyond." The face of Keith Taylor then appeared in that vision. Fred had known Keith for years, since the time they served as staff evangelists out of the same church. The only person Fred shared this revelation with was his wife, but he began to pray into it. When he heard something had broken out in Terre Haute, he sensed God say to him, "This is it. This is what I told you was coming." Fred told me, "I knew the types of meetings you and Linda had been having, and I knew what God had shown me about Keith Taylor." When Fred stepped into the meetings, all the prophetic anointing he had known was restored to him.

Often, I would say to Fred, "I believe God has given you a prophetic word for that person." Fred would feel nothing initially, but as soon as he would step in front of "that person" the prophetic word would flow. One night I watched something happen to him. When I enquired what he was experiencing he told me, "The anointing I had as a boy just returned."

Within a few weeks, Fred was joined by Kenny Knight, the pastor of a church in Paris, Illinois. I had known him for over 35 years. He has long been a one-man spiritual wrecking crew. God has used him in the word of knowledge, prophecy, and healing for years. Together, these two men modeled how to be prophets in a move of God. They were not presumptive nor pushy, but we began to recognize what I called "the look." When I would ask either of them if he had a prophetic word they would acknowledge they did but would always say, "whenever." In other words, when you feel the time is right, I will share the word the Lord has given me. Kenny, in particular, would be used in a word of knowledge. Often these words of knowledge had to do with healing. To be blunt, sometimes the revelation he was given was so specific and potentially embarrassing we were sure no one would respond to it, but then the altars would begin to fill.

In the following months and years, these two men were joined by others with a prophetic mantle - Jim Fox, Josh Hubbell, Bro.

Zimmerman and others. Additionally, the Outpouring would be visited by recognized prophets from other places. The ministry of Graham Renouf, a prophetic-pastor from New Zealand, had a huge impact on both the release of the prophetic in the house and his behind the scenes role of counsel to Outpouring pastors may be beyond calculation.

As the Outpouring developed my role went from being the evangelist to often being a teacher as well. As one visiting missionary told me, "I love this Outpouring. I love watching the power of God demonstrated throughout the service. Then you stand up and in about fifteen minutes give us a Biblical explanation of what we just experienced." She remarked how safe she felt as she watched Keith Taylor (Pastor), Fred Aguilar (Prophet), and me (Evangelist/Teacher) form a "holy huddle" on the stage. She knew we were checking out what the others sensed. We had no idea the Lord was going to continue to develop five-fold ministry in this way. We never set out to model anything. We were just seeking to follow the leadership of the Holy Spirit in each service.

At one point we invited Seth Fawcet, the lead pastor of Hope Centre in Lower Hutt, New Zealand, to speak. He leads both the church where Graham Renouf served and is the recognized leader of the Partners in Ministry, a network of Hutt Valley pastors. He is recognized locally as an apostle and is also recognized that way by the Hope Centre network that has churches in New Zealand, USA, and Europe.

It became increasingly clear to other leaders in the Terre Haute area that Keith Taylor was being given an apostolic mantle. This title was not something he gravitated toward. Indeed, he still struggles with the title. On one occasion I passed along the following counsel from Seth. "The anointing for the apostolic function increased when I embraced the responsibility of the office." Five-fold ministry is not to be considered a title to grasp but a function to flow in.

We came to realize a five-fold ministry comes out of

relationships. Teaching, good teaching, abounds about each of the offices, so we have not developed a lot of new material. During this Outpouring, we are learning how we relate to one another and flow together. Honor is significant. We are not interested in flattery, but we do seek to give genuine honor to those we minister with. Sometimes that means taking a step back so someone else can take a step forward. Outsiders were actually the first to observe how the five-fold ministry of the Holy Spirit was functioning in the Outpouring. We had not intentionally set out to function as a five-fold team. We were just flowing as the Spirit led. In hindsight, we can see how the mixes of the gifts were operating together.

In a recent conference where a dozen or so Outpouring leaders were sharing, a repeated expression occurred. More than one observed that when they were ministering now, without other members of the Outpouring being present, they felt "naked." We have come to appreciate the way the Lord uses the others. We have to trust the Holy Spirit in the lives of others. The reality is most Pentecostal preachers may function in various giftings at various times. The Holy Spirit enables us to be whatever we need to be at any particular time. However, we recognize some carry a stronger anointing than we do in certain areas. Before "the prophets" arrived at Terre Haute I often prophesied. God can still use me that way, but I rarely prophesy there now. The "A" team has arrived, so the "B" team is not needed. I was approached at a conference by the pastor of a Baptist church. "Would I pray for two of his deacons to receive the baptism in the Holy Spirit?" I carried a fair amount of administrative work in that conference, but I could have prayed for these deacons, and they would have received. However, I pointed the pastor to Jim Fox, one of the Outpouring prophets who sees a higher percentage of people filled with the Spirit than I do. I suggested he go to Jim and tell him I had sent him. An appointment was set, and in a few minutes, both deacons received a prayer language. We honor each other by allowing them to minister. We serve the King, and we serve each other.

How does this work out in an Outpouring service at Terre Haute? Apostle/Pastor Keith Taylor is in charge. We submit to him. At the same time, he is very open to other members of the five-fold group. Unless a guest speaker has been announced, I do most of the preaching at the Outpouring, and I come prepared accordingly. However, it is not unusual for a Holy Spirit intervention to adjust the meeting. We may sense one of the prophets has a word, or they may submit a word for our consideration. It is not unusual for them to submit a word to me. Keith may ask one of the teachers to share a tidbit, or he may do it himself. Altar ministry may flow out of either a prophetic word or the preached word. In either event, most altar ministry will involve the local Cross Tabernacle prayer team and/or the five-fold Outpouring preachers in attendance at the meeting. Souls are always a high priority. Personal ministry time usually occurs. God's Manifest Presence has continued to set the Outpouring apart from just a church meeting.

One example of flowing together in five-fold ministry occurred in Baguio, Philippines, where the Outpouring team was leading evangelistic meetings. Randall Burton, the apostle/pastor, from Northview Church in Columbus, Indiana, was preaching. At the close of his message, without warning, he called me to the stage to give a salvation altar call. Over 400 responded to that invitation. Later, Prophet Fred Aguilar simply said, "We understand you carry an anointing for the salvation invitation that we do not carry."

Relationship … flow … honor … trust are key words in the developing five-fold ministry. We do not claim to be the final word on this. We are growing together with the desire to see His Kingdom extended.

In a recent conversation with Keith Taylor, he observed that the whole concept of five-fold ministry is revolutionizing his church. Children's ministry, music ministry, and youth ministry are all beginning to take on a five-fold team look. The superman concept is being replaced with a team approach. An "apostle" is still in place, but the flow is more through a team of committed followers of Jesus.

The Role of Prayer

During the early weeks of the Outpouring, we were joined by Marvin Adams who served as the leader of a House of Prayer. After a few minutes of sitting next to me, he turned and said to me, "Count me in, I recognize this." I discovered that during the 1990s he had been on staff at a church in the Chicago area that had been significantly touched by the Toronto Outpouring. For several years he had been involved with the International House of Prayer in Kansas City. So, he was both a revivalist and a prayer movement participant. For the next two to three years the House of Prayer in Terre Haute became a significant intercessor for us personally and for the Outpouring. The location of their building was not far from where Linda and I were being housed, so it was not unusual for us to slip into a prayer session. At its peak, this House of Prayer was praying nearly twelve hours a day. At first, we would remain incognito. Eventually, we could no longer do that. So, while Marvin respected our privacy, they would also often pray for us when we were in attendance. During that season they outgrew their facilities twice. Once a month we relocated the Outpouring service to their facilities. Their building would be packed as people came from many different congregations to pray. Those meetings would be led by a combination of their team and the leadership of the Outpouring. Actually, the meetings were being led by the Holy Spirit. There was no official order of service. We simply joined together and allowed the Spirit to lead. Often, I would serve as an almost secret "clearing-house" for those who had a sense of direction or input for those prayer gatherings. This unique prayer partnership was significant for both the local church and the larger city. They served as primary intercessors until God increased the level of intercession within Cross Tabernacle itself. Even in revival, things change. Eventually, that prayer ministry felt led to a new focus, and its director was led by God to relocate to another city and plant a prayer ministry there.

I will forever be grateful for the season with them.

Local pastors in Terre Haute have prayed together for many years. Every Wednesday morning a group of evangelical and Pentecostal pastors come together to pray. They have been doing this for over fifteen years at this writing. This group is a part of the larger ministerial group within the city. That group also prays together. Most of the local preachers who are a part of the Outpouring participate in both of these prayer groups. Additionally, they meet together every Thursday morning to pray, prophesy, and otherwise minister to each other and discuss Outpouring related themes. Terre Haute is also the home city for a national prayer ministry led by David Butts, who is a part of the National Day of Prayer Team. Initially, the House of Prayer hosted the Thursday morning group, but after that season ended another pastor opened his place for the group to meet and pray.

Intercessory prayer has not been without its problems. I think it would be fair to say the Brownsville Revival brought intercession out of the closet for many churches. In some places, this was hugely significant, while in other places it was problematic. Intercessors tragically have been known to split churches. This checkered history has made pastors cautious regarding the developing of intercessors in their churches.

We knew the Outpouring in Terre Haute could not depend solely upon the prayer of the International House of Prayer team located in Terre Haute. Indeed, God began to raise up a team of intercessors within Cross Tabernacle. Initially, it was hand-picked by the church pastor and functioned solely on Facebook, but when he felt the time was right, the team began to have face to face meetings. God had prepared a lady within the church to help facilitate that team. In addition to that group, which still functions in the shadows, the church has a Sunday morning 9:00 am prayer service and a Tuesday morning prayer service.

As one national prayer ministry moved off the scene, as far as the Outpouring is concerned, another moved in. The Lord sent a seasoned couple, Brian and Denise Shaw, back to Terre Haute after they had ministered for years alongside national ministries in Tulsa, Oklahoma, and Branson, Missouri. In addition to participating in the Pastors' prayer groups, they have begun a Saturday school of prayer that rotates among several churches who are a part of the Outpouring. They have intensified the prayer ministry in the city. At this writing, their ministry is expanding both within the city, the larger Outpouring circle, and beyond.

Concentric Circles

I have watched what I describe as concentric circles develop within the Outpouring. Initially, this was a single church revival. While every department and age group within the church was significantly touched (at one point, youth group attendance was up 500%), the pastor observed the impact was particularly significant for those aged 35 and below. This group had heard about revival but had little personal experience with it. I have often heard it said twenties and thirties are not interested in revival. I can only say that has not been our experience in Terre Haute. They signed on big time, and now their children are growing up as children of the Outpouring.

As reports began to filter out, regional churches and/or pastors began to participate. Randall Burton and many from his church would drive two hours to attend the services. Now his own church has been in an Outpouring for five-plus years. Kenny Knight began to bring his people from Paris, Illinois, which is about 30 minutes away by car. While Randall pastors an Assemblies of God church, Kenny pastors a Word of Faith Church. Marvin McCormick followed my mother as a pastor of an evangelical church about an hour north of Terre Haute. He began attending regularly with my mother and a group of hungry people. People from Robinson, Illinois, about an hour south began to attend.

The internet played a large role. Cross Tabernacle has been live streaming services for years. Some services have been viewed by several thousand people. In the early months of the Outpouring, we received reports from the Panera ladies from Ohio. Two ladies were going to Panera Bread, so they could go online and watch the services. I received testimonies from as far as New Zealand and the Philippines of people who were watching online. Pastors within the state of Indiana began watching, and at least one of these reported being healed while participating in a service online.

At one point, Carey Robertson, who had served as the senior associate pastor of the Brownsville Revival, shared his belief that God had tossed a pebble into the middle of the USA and the ripple effects were going to be much larger than we realized.

What had begun as a local church revival was now impacting hungry people from the region. Then the impact began to move to the local pastors. Several began to attend services on a regular basis. The Lord told one hungry pastor He was going to send him to a city of revival. Shortly after that, he was invited to pastor in Terre Haute. They have become an Outpouring fixture. One of the staff pastors from Cross Tabernacle was invited to pastor Victory Christian Centre on the east side of Terre Haute. That church has now been impacted by the Outpouring. Its pastoral team is a part of the larger Outpouring team. That church conducts an annual tent outreach where Outpouring preachers preach. The local Teen Challenge director made Outpouring attendance a requirement for its residents. So many lives have been transformed. That director is now pastoring a church in a city about three hours south of Terre Haute. There are early indicators of something significant developing in that city.

In any given Outpouring service 15-50 preachers will show up. Relationships are developing. Many of them are now preaching for each other. In a recent conference at least 100 preachers were in one service.

Transforming the Preacher

In fact, the transformation of preachers and the developing of five-fold relationships is one of the biggest stories of the Outpouring. Several preachers have personally thanked me for the Outpouring and its impact upon their personal lives and ministries. As a result of the Outpouring, preaching schedules are more filled than ever before for some preachers. Both regional and now international ministry has developed for a number of preachers connected to the Outpouring. One found himself preaching a six-month revival in southern Illinois. During that season, he told me it was his experiences at Cross Tabernacle that enabled him to lead that revival.

I would love to point to a specific sermon I preached that transformed the lives and ministries of these preachers. The reality is I cannot do that. The transformation came as they stood night after night at the altar in the Presence of God. I believe it was the manifest Presence of God more than anything else that contributed to the transformation of these preachers. Additionally, relationships are developing between them. We are probably too early in this season of revival to know where it is going to go, but one leader from the state of Missouri who is being impacted by the Terre Haute Outpouring has called it the most life-changing thing he has ever been a part of.

Outpouring Must Include
Outreaches/Hubs of Revival

One of the concerns of past revivals has been that many are inward focused. One pastor of a church in the mid-west that experienced revival in the 1990s indicated its demise was connected to the fact they turned it inward rather than outward. God's purpose in revival has always been the lost. One missionary asked me how the Terre Haute revival was impacting evangelism?

First, Cross Tabernacle has always been evangelistic. Outreach has always been a part of the church. They participate in city-wide parades; they do a "Joy Dish Washing Soap" distribution in poor neighborhoods annually, the annual single parents Christmas event ministers to single parents and children, they do events in neighborhood parks. Feeding of the poor and disadvantaged is a part of what they do.

For nearly a dozen years, I have been connected to a conference near Chicago, Illinois, where for most of this time I served as its co-host. About three or four years ago Outpouring preachers began attending this conference. The theme of the conference for the past several years has been the Glory.

As the Outpouring preachers began attending this conference, cross-pollination began to occur. Dr. James Horvath, host of the conference, leads Calvary Lighthouse Church in Rochelle, Illinois. For years, he has been doing city-wide evangelistic crusades in the Philippines. A partnership developed between the Road to Glory Conference and the Outpouring. In 2015, the Outpouring team joined with Dr. James Horvath in doing city-wide crusades in the Philippines. We participated in simultaneous crusades in multiple sites in Manila and then in multiple cities. The reports are that scores of thousands of people met Jesus. In 2016 the team returned to the Philippines to minister specifically to the pastors of Baguio.

As I write, this the team is in the planning stages of a similar event in Northern Ireland. Plans are to do simultaneous events across Ireland and then close with a huge outreach in Belfast.

Cross Tabernacle itself took a team from the church to assist in evangelizing first nations people in the southwest of the USA. The "Revive Indiana" team also came to Terre Haute. Its stress on personal evangelism blended well with what God was doing in the city. Teams from the Outpouring still go out into the city on nearly a weekly basis.

Relationships between churches have also been developing. Some are calling these churches hubs of revival. A clear relationship developed between Cross Tabernacle in Terre Haute and Northview Church in Columbus, Indiana. Parishioners began attending outpouring services held in the other church. Rochelle, Illinois became another hub. Conferences at one church were attended by people from all three churches. Input from and relationship with Belfast, Northern Ireland has created a relationship with another hub church. Several other churches are relating at some level to the Outpouring in Terre Haute. I am hesitant to even begin mentioning other cities and churches for fear I will overlook some. Outpouring preachers have ministered in hungry churches across Indiana and to a lesser extent surrounding states. Some of those cities and churches appear to be in the early stages of something significant. However, it is too early to know for certain how far this Outpouring may go. Prophecies continue to suggest "we have not seen anything yet." By nature, I am somewhat conservative, so I am more prepared to report than project, but this has become the biggest thing I have personally been involved with.

My eschatology allows for a "last days revival." My heart burns for even more. We rejoice in reports from other places. We welcome the Holy Spirit! I believe you welcome Him too!

11

HOW TO PASTOR A REVIVAL:
INTERVIEWS WITH REVIVAL LEADERS

In the 1990s several revival centers were hosting conferences on revival. Their theme largely had to do with the early chapters of this book, "How do we attract the Presence of God?" I remember a conversation I had with a denominational leader who described the mid-nineties as one of the most exciting times to be a denominational leader in his state. Every phone call seemed to bring another report of revival breaking out in another church. However, the reality of the nineties was that revival ended for most of the churches that had experienced it. It became a part of their history, but not a part of their DNA.

So, I ask the question, "How does one successfully pastor revival or outpouring?" As an evangelist who has been a part of a number of significant moves of God I could offer my own perspective, but I thought it would be of greater interest to get the thoughts of pastors who have piloted their churches in the white water of revival. So, this chapter will consist of a series of interviews I did with such pastors. I am going to approach this chapter as if we were sitting together in a room and these spiritual leaders were responding to my questions. Let me begin by introducing the participants. I think it is fair to say I have a unique relationship with each of these men.

Seth Fawcet has been the lead pastor at Hope Centre in Lower Hutt, New Zealand, since the mid-nineties. Prior to that, he served on the staff of that church. As mentioned earlier, I personally preached a 20-week meeting in 2000 at his church and a seventeen-week city wide meeting in 2001 where his church was the foundation for the meetings.

Graham Renouf served as the senior associate pastor at Hope Centre for much of the last fifteen years. He has just stepped down from a full-time position to give more time to itinerant ministry. In the early 90s, the church he was leading in the town of Dannevirke experienced a revival, so that he will speak from both situations.

Tony Collis serves as the lead pastor of the Hope Centre in Levin, New Zealand. In 2008 he was the lead pastor of the Assemblies of God church in the same town. During that time, I preached a nineteen-week revival at his church.

Randall Burton is the lead pastor of Northview Church (Assemblies of God) in Columbus, Indiana, which he founded more than 20 years ago. He is also the author of a revival book entitled "River Rising" published by Evergreen Press. Although I had preached for him earlier in 2010, it was the Outpouring in Terre Haute that catalyzed what God is doing in his church. He has been in revival since 2011 or so.

Keith Taylor is the lead pastor at Cross Tabernacle in Terre Haute, Indiana. He has served in that role for 20 years. This is the church where I have been preaching Outpouring services since 2010.

The Stories Behind the Stories

Michael Livengood: We often describe revival/outpouring as a sovereign move of the Spirit of God, and I fully support this description. However, such a description does not suggest revival occurs in a vacuum. There is always a story behind the story. That story includes events going on in the life of the leader of a revival as well as in the church. In your case what was happening personally before the revival/outpouring took place?

Seth Fawcet: In the 80s I was the youth leader at Hutt Christian Covenant Centre. During that season we began experiencing a move of God which led into some extended meetings with an evangelist. Our church had a Pentecostal heritage but not a revival practice. Meetings were stopped, and the question became "Why did we stop?" This motivated me to be careful not to close meetings too soon. People often stop too soon because of a failure to see the big picture. The reasons seemed valid at the time, but in hindsight, they were not as important as the revival. Another important moment for me was the decision to leave a secular career to pastor the same church. At the time I was among the top wage earners in New Zealand. So, the call of God brought a sense of expectation in my life.

Another thing was the willingness to be a fool for Christ. I was challenged with "Am I willing to be a fool for Him?" The Lord was teaching me how to be countercultural. For example, in the Kiwi (New Zealand) culture, boys do not cry, but it was an important part of my journey to learn how to be countercultural. People often resist when something is countercultural. Teaching people to yield to the Spirit is challenging.

Keith Taylor: My grandfather was a Church of God, Cleveland, Tennessee evangelist. He passed away when I was very young, but before his death, he imparted this calling into my life. My grandmother continued to nurture and seed the calling of God into me until she also passed away, and then that impartation set upon my wife, oil anointing and all! She continued praying until I finally submitted to the call on my life.

During this time, I had an open vision. I could see a church service and the back of a preacher; this was a few years before I stepped into God's call, and I was not totally living right. In fact, when this vision occurred I was sitting at the kitchen table with my guitar and writing music. Suddenly, I was thrust into the vision, and I chased that vision for many, many years.

The 1996 Brownsville Revival totally changed the direction of my life. We stepped out of the pastorate and into evangelism. The anointing changed; passion, drive, and vision changed. During that time, I had yet another daytime vision of change coming in God's anointing on my life. This was as I was driving with my wife on Interstate 70 after a Sunday morning service at Abundant Life Worship Center in Clay City, Indiana. I suddenly saw an angel descending from the sky, look at me, bend down and open a large wooden chest. As soon as the chest was opened what looked like golden smoke and flakes suddenly came rushing upward out of it, and as soon as this took place, the angel spoke and told me this was for me, that "From this point on your anointing and direction has changed."

Sometime after that, I was attending a service with the Brownsville team in Cleveland, Tennessee. The church was full to overflowing, and I was unable to get into the building. However, the church air conditioner broke down, and they opened the windows to provide ventilation. A pastor named Carlos Cox and I went to a window covered by a pine tree. As we stepped into that area, it was like a private closet. We hung in that window and listened to that meeting for over four hours. Suddenly we somehow found ourselves standing in the altar area, and I still do not know how that happened. Pastor John Kilpatrick and Evangelist Steve Hill laid hands on us and prayed; that's all I remember for some time. A few days after that meeting God opened doors for me to step out of pastoring the Clay City Church of God and into full-time evangelism. This, in turn, was a set up for me after a few years to take up the pastorate of Terre Haute First Assembly of God, now called Cross Tabernacle, where I have just stepped into my 19th year as pastor.

Graham Renouf: I had come to a place where there was a

desperate hunger within me. I knew it was God, but I did not know what I was looking for, and I was still not satisfied. My wife and I knew we were called to pastor, but we did not want to do church as we had been doing it before. I knew from Scripture there was so, so much more than we were seeing. I decided to press into God by increasing my prayer life. I began to spend three hours at the church in prayer four or five days a week from 9.00 am to noon. After about 20 minutes of this I would feel prayed out, so I would go into speaking in other tongues. I still felt a lot of frustration, but God encouraged me to keep going. During this time there were encounters with the Lord that would keep me focused.

After I had finished a pastoral visit one day, the Lord said to me, "You can build the church your way, or you can build the church my way. You can build a church with your skills, or you can chase me. and I will teach you the Kingdom." He went on to say, "Your way will work for a season, but the foundation is poor. My way will build a stronger foundation, but it will be harder because it will cost you your life and because it will be built in intimacy." Two weeks after that I had a repeat encounter as I was driving where God asked me, "Have you made up your mind yet?" I had to pull over to the side of the road to weep. About that time my wife and I learned to pray without ceasing. If Paul could do that, we figured we could learn to do that too. A season of revival came to the church. It lasted about three years or so. It was the sweetest time of our life. But with that revival came a number of issues. [Those issues will be shared later in this chapter]. As a result of those issues, I had no interest in revival any longer. I had been hurt, and I wanted nothing to do with it.

In 2000 while I was ministering in the Hutt Valley at a Presbyterian Church I was told about a revival that was happening at Hutt Christian Covenant Center ([now Hope Centre). Curiosity brought me. I came very late to the meeting, and when I saw the clothing and the hats (Smith Wigglesworth type of hats) people were wearing, I thought for sure I was in the wrong church. I told the Lord

I had already seen this before and turned to leave, but Pastor Seth Fawcet stopped me and asked if he could pray for me. When he did, I hit the floor, which I did not like. My heart had just been touched, and I did not want that to happen, but I knew immediately this was what I had been looking for. When I crawled to my feet, I went straight to Seth and said, "Why you...why here...why now?" He said he did not have an answer to that question, but he and Michael Livengood prayed for me again, and I was wasted for three hours. That encounter ruined me for life.

Randall Burton: In a nutshell, at that time I was feeling real loneliness and despair. We had gone through a church split or a church splinter. Our church had been growing numerically, but I felt disconnected from other ministers and ministry. I felt like we were just going through the motions, and because of the church issues, I was having a bit of a struggle personally. I felt like I had no sense of a spiritual father. In fact, I felt like a spiritual orphan. I asked God, "Why don't I have a spiritual father?" His response was to tell me, "Be the father you did not have, and I will take care of the rest." I attempted to do this, but honestly, I still felt empty.

In early 2010 we took time off to go to California. We were asking ourselves a series of questions. "Who are we? What are we doing?" During this sabbatical, the Lord said to me, "You are anointed wherever you go or whatever you do." But I discovered this did not mean God was validating all the actions we might take. I then spoke to my District Superintendent (state denominational leader) about what was going on because I still felt a need for more. I was looking for counsel. He connected me to Michael Livengood, who began to answer the questions of who I am and the desire for a spiritual father. During that critical time in my life, I found both destiny and fathering. That phone call changed my life. Really, it was like critical mass had been reached for me.

Tony Collis: I was freaking out. I had been involved in planting house churches in both Asia and New Zealand. I was quite happy with what we were doing, but we received a prophetic word about a left turn. The Lord told us to close doors on what we were doing. I felt the pastor at Levin was going to ask us to come and help them on staff at the church, which he did. God made it clear we were to go and work with them. For two years we were on staff and knew the pastoral baton was to be passed on to us. We knew we were in the right place, but we had no idea what was going on.

Michael Livengood: Tony, in 2000 and 2001 you were an itinerant evangelist. You and your wife were a part of the meetings in Hutt Valley. Can you talk to us about that season?

Tony Collis: Those meetings were life changing! God was doing stuff I had never experienced before…supernatural stuff. Lynette, my wife, was going to meeting after meeting and receiving prayer in every meeting. She was transformed in front of me. She had always been supportive and looked after the children while I traveled and preached. I felt to strongly encourage her to attend the meetings, and I stayed home to take care of the kids. Those meetings were a huge boost for Lynette. I saw her transformed. She became so hungry for the things of God. She was walking in a new authority with a pursuit of God. Her joy exploded. Some nights she would come home from the revival services, and when she would get into bed, it began shaking. Some of this was way outside of my box, but I could not deny the signature of God all over it. I experienced encounter upon encounter. I guess you could say we became victims of our revival experience. It changed how we saw ministry and life.

Michael Livengood: I am a little blown away with some of your personal stories. Wow! Let's shift from personal experiences and talk about your churches. What was going on in your church prior to revival breaking out in it?

Seth Fawcet: There was an expectation that God was going to do something. You cannot go into revival without a sense of being called. People who enter revival out of soul get burned out. We started holding a Saturday night prayer and worship time from 6:30 for one hour. (As already mentioned, the church had a history of prayer, including a fifty-year 24/7 prayer meeting). We would worship for twenty minutes or so and then began laying hands on people to receive Holy Spirit baptism and freedom in the Spirit. The goal was to see people filled with and be fluent in the Spirit. We did these meetings for two years.

We had heard about revival, although we had not seen it, so we were going after it. In those meetings as well as others I told revival stories. At first, these were stories from other places until God gave us our own stories. The telling of these "God stories" created hunger within the people. Culture is created by thoughts and words. By telling these revival stories, we made revival normal, rather than something seen as abnormal. Too many places see revival as abnormal. This was a case of redefining normal for us. We also began putting up big banners with revival themes such as "Lord we have heard of your fame." Revival slogans and language became a part of the church's culture.

We were building hunger. Hunger for revival comes from the pastor and leadership. The pastor must model this. If the pastor is not hungry, revival will not come, even if the people are hungry for it. Too many moves of God are stymied because of the comfort zone of the leaders. Leadership is not always comfortable because leaders are always going into new territory. As a leader, I had to be prepared to pay whatever price was necessary for a move of God. A commitment to the journey became essential. Sometimes even family and friends will not understand what is in your heart. For me, I believed you would never make progress until the pain of the known or the pain of the status quo is greater than the pain of the unknown. I understood some moves of the Spirit are countercultural, but isn't Christianity supposed to be a counter-culture? We must accept that before revival comes. Revival will never fit inside of the existing church culture.

We began training key people in the things of the Spirit. We were blessed in New Zealand with the ministry material of New Zealand evangelist Bill Subritsky. We took advantage of his insights to train people. We were preparing the way of the Lord by removing the obstacles. Some of those things we had to deal with were spiritual pride and questions like "What is the point of this?" or statements like "But we have seen this before." We really had to work on the buy-in. Because of the move among youth in the 80s they had a taste for revival that could be built upon. This was a key. The under 30s were not so set in their ways that they could not be molded.

Keith Taylor: Before I was called to be the pastor of First Assembly of God, which is now called Cross Tabernacle, a prayer meeting was held. A prophetic word was given from Isaiah chapter 54 about enlarging the tent. The message God gave me for the Sunday I candidated was from the same text. About three months into being the pastor the Lord woke me with instructions to come to the church sanctuary for prayer. He spoke to me that to those who would seek Him he would give His glory. About six months later Fred Aguilar prophesied "Can you hear the cry, the cry of the one who is to give birth? The time of delivery is nigh for the midwife to give birth. The husband is enlarging the house to make room. There are many who will be delivered! Prepare thyself, prepare thyself, prepare thyself, for they shall come! It is time to prepare!" I felt led to call the pastoral staff, deacons, and spouses to accountability.

I think it is fair to say much of the journey from then until 2010 was all to do with preparation. A variety of guest speakers would be used by God to reinforce the prophetic word. We were led to establish a variety of ministries to the community…Teen Challenge…Single Parents Christmas…walking in the Drunk Parade (Homecoming parade for Indiana State University)…Chi Alpha campus ministry…airing of our services by TBN…providing the police department with Bibles… prison ministries… to name a few. Former pastor and mentor Jack Macintosh shared a dream God gave him about an oil well bubbling up in our foyer. The oil was loaded into train tankers which were backed up to the church. That oil was taken throughout the world. At first, we thought the fulfillment of that dream was internet ministry. The streaming of our services has gone worldwide with some services being viewed 10,000 times. Now, we realize it was larger than we thought. In January of 2010, we joined nine other churches in a city wide Divine Experiment. We were fasting and praying for a city-wide Presence of God. The closer we got to August 2010 we sensed transformation was in the air. Then you came to preach in August. After a week of meetings, you went to Germany. I heard about the Bay of the Spirit revival in Mobile, Alabama and felt led to take the staff down there. During that meeting, the Lord spoke to me about the third service and told me that I would know then if this was the season for the fulfillment of the promise. I asked you if you could return to be here for that service. On that day it became evident this was the season.

Graham Renouf: The church in Dannevirke had gone through a split a few years before I became the pastor. Allegations of sexual abuse and more were brought against people in the church, which had become a shadow of its former self. The previous pastor was still there. During this season there was still a measure of presence and atmosphere; there was a willingness to go after God. Then the pastor left, another came for two years, and then he left too. By then the church had dwindled to a relatively small group who asked me to become the pastor. The manifest Presence of God became our primary objective, although we did not use that term then.

We learned that if the leader does not pursue the Presence of God the people will not pursue it either. Worship reached a new height, and that was followed by miracles. The Dannevirke break was on a wintry Wednesday night. When I left the building after a prayer meeting, I discovered my people outside on the ground in the frost crying out to God. Prayer meeting had been attended by only me and one other person for over a year, and then within months, every family was represented. This happened without pressure to attend the meeting. The stories from the prayer meeting grew hunger. Hunger was fundamental. Nobody wanted to return to the past. We were a broken people that God had put hunger into. He had to birth it. Passages like Jeremiah 29:11 and 2 Chronicles 7:14 were important to us.

Michael Livengood: The revival you have been sharing with us actually occurred in Dannevirke, New Zealand in the early 90s. Is that correct?

Graham Renouf: Yes. This happened about three years before the Toronto Outpouring, so we did not even know what that was. At the time we had little understanding of what we were experiencing.

Randall Burton: I was born again in a revival in a Baptist church and filled with the Holy Spirit in another revival. After yielding to the call to ministry, the training I had for ministry included learning a variety of then current church trends. We planted the church in 1995. In the planting, we looked at various models such as Courageous Leadership, Purpose Driven Churches and so on. We developed a hybrid church where we were sort of between seeker sensitive and purpose driven with a desire to be Spirit open. We were a church driven by horizontal relationships more than the vertical relationship. We were highly relational as a church. We had lots of programs, and we were way ahead of the times with our use of media. In hindsight, we had lots of appearance but no substance. Then we went through a painful church split. The split forced me to reassess our church, and I realized we had lost the vertical.

Tony Collis: During my years as an itinerant evangelist I would speak at Levin Assembly of God from time to time. It was one of those places where you would catch a whiff of something special that God wanted to do there. So, when I became the senior leader, I had an anticipation of something about to happen.

Prayer became a priority for us. The men especially were key in this. We had been involved in what had been a very vital ministry. We had seen thousands of house churches planted. I strongly believed God had not moved us to Levin to become just an average pastor of an average church. So, I was expecting something special. Our years of ministry among house churches gave me a love for the

145

small, while my experience with congregational based revival gave me a love for the big.

So, we were full of hunger and expectation, but I will have to say I had no real realization of what was going to happen. On that Sunday you preached for us the whiff of the oily rag of revival was there.

Michael Livengood: OK, we have looked a bit at your personal background and a bit of what was going on in your church before revival came. Let's talk more specifically about the revival or outpouring in your church. Can you name two to four things that seemed to be important to bringing revival in your church?

Keith Taylor: First, prayer was the key. This included both personal and corporate prayer. For 19 years I have been led to be on the church property between 4.00 am and 4:30 am on Sunday mornings praying and anointing the property with oil. Not only did I practice prayer personally, but I was led to teach and lead the church into a weekly prayer service.

Michael Livengood: Let me interject for a moment regarding two things. I understand the importance you place on anointing with oil. I am aware you anoint every pew with oil personally. I found that out by laying my hands on those same pews and discovering the oil (Laugh out loud). I would also observe that your weekly prayer service at 9.00 am on Sunday morning is one of the most effective prayer services I have been involved with.

Keith Taylor: I believe the unction in the pulpit was also important. Solid Holy Ghost led preaching and teaching sets in place deep conviction and hunger for righteousness. I believe it births action in the pews and a heart for the lost in the people. It imparts a hunger for discipleship.

The third element and this is so important, is atmosphere or God's Glory Presence. Perhaps we can explore what creates atmosphere later.

The fourth element I would suggest is something I call "organic placement." This is where hands-on evangelism unfolds in the midst of the people. Ministries both inside and outside the body take place. These are Holy Spirit initiated and operate with a five-fold foundation, direction, and spiritual oversight.

Graham Renouf: I don't think there is any question about this for me. Hunger and prayer were the two key things for us. What you focus your attention on through the eye gate and ear gate is very important. I was reading books looking for answers to the cry in my heart. God began to bring to my attention stories of historical revival.

Michael Livengood: Were those stories you read only for yourself?

Graham Renouf: No, I began sharing those revival stories with my people. I shared with them what I was discovering. I was reading about the Argentine revival, the Welsh revival, and the Azusa Street revival. Neither Toronto nor Brownsville had broken out yet. I was reading about men God used in the past. I found books that a church was chucking out (throwing out). Men like William Branham, Smith Wigglesworth, Evan Roberts, William Seymour and others. I know that Branham went off the rails at one point, but God spoke to me through the ministry of his early days. Reading these stories fed my hunger. Sharing them became hugely important for the church. Our hunger led to prayer. I will never stop talking about revival; it fans the fire.

Randall Burton: That hunger thing Graham is speaking of resonates with me. I think the first thing that was important for me was simple desperation. I had reached the place of me becoming nothing for Him to be something. Before revival, I announced to the church I was coming out of the closet. I told them I was going back to my revival roots.

Another pre-revival for me was to connect with the right people. The Lord brought into my life people like Michael Livengood, Graham Renouf, who unpacked prophetic and worship teams for us, Fred Aguilar, who would help bring revival to the church. I learned that revival brings challenge. Graham, like a father, talked about where we were and where we were going. He encouraged me that we had the goods...don't drop the ball between meetings.

I think that attending the revival which became the Terre Haute Outpouring was very important for me and then for all the church. Attending the outpouring at Terre Haute not only imparted or released something inside of me but it also brought an introduction to Keith Taylor who has become both a mentor and a close friend. Those relationships introduced me to the Road to Glory Conference in Rochelle, Illinois, which challenged me to go from visitation to habitation, to become a glory filled church. I met people like the Dunlop brothers from Northern Ireland who sharpened my understanding of prophetic and apostolic ministry.

Yes, I would say personal desperation and right connections. I needed to become connected to those who were further into the river than I was. That messed up my denominational hairdo. God had to allow me to wallow on the floor because that was where His life was. He was "on the floor." So, God put me on the floor. God had to get me drunk and messed up. It was important that I understood I was not the pope of church life.

Michael Livengood: Obviously, I believe that revival is the most wonderful thing that can happen in the life of a local church. However, revival is not without its challenges. I once spoke to pastors at a revival conference on the good, the bad, and the ugly of revival. What would be some of the biggest obstacles you faced to either the arrival or the sustaining of revival?

Seth Fawcet: People will filter what happens through the soul, forgetting that spirit is contrary to soul. Teaching is required to help people learn to yield to spirit rather than soul.

Voices of opposition will arise during revival. Often these voices are more concerned about the comfort of the soul than the progress of the spirit. This is a major challenge for pastors. Many will give the voice of soul greater prominence than the voice of spirit. Often, we are more programmed to listen to the voice of the soul. Pastors are often programmed to do exactly that.

A third obstacle is listening to the wrong voices within the church and within a network/denomination. We saw that jealousy arose in some quarters, especially the network, or perhaps it could be better understood as misunderstandings on the part of the "opposition." People want God to move, but we want Him to bless what we are doing rather than doing what God is blessing. We must adjust to the Spirit and not require the Spirit to adjust to us.

Keith Taylor: Oh my! Here are some things we have dealt with. An immediate demonic, religious, critical spirit will surface and always be a factor. Carnal activity within the church also surfaces. By that, I mean hidden sins, old wineskin mentality, comfort zone protection, ownership mentality. This will especially manifest within those who were raised in the current atmosphere before Glory broke out. You will need to prepare your people for demonic buffeting of the saints hungry for more of God.

Don't be surprised at the constant maintenance in the area of praise and worship. There will be a constant flesh versus spirit battle. The enemy will look for anything he can use to stop the flow of Outpouring, anything to break the cadence of the Holy Spirit anointing, anything to stop a breakthrough in praise and a warring worship.

Revival also brings constant financial challenges in many areas. For example, in the early days of the Outpouring, we had to replace major air conditioning units. More use of the building brings greater building maintenance issues and other increased challenges.

Another issue is the length of services and the number of them. I call it the demonic awareness of time. How many services; when and how do we adjust the schedule?

Closely related to this is the challenge of keeping church life healthy. As a pastor, you will be concerned about the daily needs of the church. A part of this is learning how to structure the Outpouring culture into the body. This, of course, will bring growing pains. Some of these will be good and some bad, but it will be a part of the journey. Sifting does and will take place in the church. Praying for Godly wisdom became a priority.

We found revival brought community awareness in totally different areas. The religious community may respond with jealous spirits and anti-Christ spirits. Some parts of the evangelical community, for example, responded very negatively to our speaking in unknown tongues. But we also experienced other positives like hunger. A city church heart will come forth. A greater unity and agreement will manifest itself by an awareness and activation of unified prayer times. I have been praying for over fifteen years with a number of both evangelical and Pentecostal pastors. Not only has that continued, but additional prayer meetings within the Pentecostal preachers have developed. Not everyone will get on board but work with those who will.

Graham Renouf: My first response was to think of the wet blankets that can come into our lives and tempt us to let the fire go out. We must not stop praying, chasing, and telling stories during the hard times until we reach the exit of the valley.

The revival in Dannevirke did blow apart. As I look back, I think one of the biggest obstacles was that I did not know how to be the new wineskin that could carry and maintain the new wine. You know the teaching behind new wineskin versus old wineskin. We were probably impacted by a lack of knowledge. I assumed this new revival would be my life forever. I felt like I was not walking in an earthly realm, but in a heavenly one already. While I do believe God intends this as a normal lifestyle, there is more to that than just desiring it.

Let me try to explain what happened to us. The "suddenly" for us was like an initial explosion of a gas container. We carried on in the energy of that explosion for a few months. Then it began to taper, for lack of a better word. I do not believe God intends for a revival to get derailed. How we handle that taper is very important. Even during revival life will go on within what God is doing...family life...pastoral care. But that petrol bomb feels all consuming.

Nothing else matters. We did not want to leave services even at 2.00 am. But tiredness does come in, and you have to balance the desire for the petrol bomb with the realities of life and Kingdom building. Religious, pharisaical thinking and so forth kept getting in the way. We had to adjust to the new thing God was doing. Professionalism is dangerous. Some of this thinking begins to kill the move of God. How do we become new wineskins? Certain things in revival cannot be placed in a box.

One obstacle we faced was the children's church workers growing tired of looking after kids and feeling like they were missing the move of God. We tried to set in place a plan where the workers ministered to the kids for one hour and then the parents were to take responsibility. But the parents were so lost in God the kids almost got killed. Our church was on a main road, and one night one of the little girls who was no longer being watched over was caught attempting to cross that road. Some stranger stopped her and brought her back into the church. Structure is necessary, but the danger is in driving people, and we began to struggle with spirit versus flesh.

We experienced the danger of neglecting basics such as cell group meetings. One challenge was balancing the need for fellowship with revival.

Some people will leave the church, which causes a Pastor to become concerned because of this loss. Pastors need to help people understand the purposes of God. Sometimes people want only the joy without responsibility. So, we must teach them how to balance the two. Stubbornness and being unteachable have an impact.

Another issue is the temptation to drive rather than lead. Self-centeredness, is my own spiritual gratification becoming more important than the welfare of the church. There is a danger of wearing people out.

There is also a danger of turning revival into an event rather than having the Presence. We struggled to find the balance of not burning out versus the danger of distraction and losing momentum.

The Wow Factor

Sometimes to avoid wearing people out we run the risk of losing momentum. Balancing this is huge.

We learned it is not enough to keep a form of revival and lose the substance. It is always man that hinders the move of God. We have to be prepared to admit we do not know all of the answers.

Randall Burton: Revival itself became an obstacle. By that, I mean understanding the terminology. We had to help people's understanding of certain terms. The word revival can become an issue. I searched the Scriptures to get a better handle on what was happening to us so that I could explain it to our people. For us, Outpouring must become "who we are" not "what we do." I personally cannot live without this! This is my DNA. Reading the revivalists helped me.

My personal inability to understand what was happening was an obstacle. Honestly, this is where people like you, Michael, were a big help. You provide language that can help us to understand. I found a lot of people were making river noises, but they were not going deep themselves. Unless you are swimming in the river yourself, you cannot understand the sound, the depth. Deep calls unto deep at the noise of your waterfalls. You cannot take people where you have not gone yourself. Guides know the river better than the tourists they are leading. It is one thing to go to the altar of repentance and another thing to take people beyond that into the depth God wants them to go. You can read about revival to the point where you sound like an expert, but knowing about revival does not mean you are experiencing revival. I discovered that information is not impartation. Reading without activating does not produce revival. Activating includes starting where you are and beginning to practice the Presence of God.

I discovered that you cannot teach people from the river bank. There are no lifeguards on a river bank because the river is always moving. You cannot teach people how to swim without getting into the water yourself. Trial and error are important. Check the clothes of your leaders. Are they getting wet themselves? Your history is a

152

predictor of revival.

Tony Collis: I came to realize there will be surges of the Spirit resulting in a real manifestation of the flesh. The atmosphere of revival confronts works of flesh and brings scum to the surface. A real process of sanctification was taking place, and this work was happening in me as well. This brought a growing gap between those moving forward and those occupying only the ground where they stood. As a pastor I wanted everyone involved, but sadly some decided to say "No," and that decision became the beginning of the place of two camps. Some began to say, "Who are all these new people? Why do we have to have all these new people?" ...As if it was an evil thing.

Michael Livengood: I have a feeling that some of these very transparent things you gentlemen have shared will be interesting and helpful to other pastors and leaders as they traverse the white water of revival. Let's move on to a slightly different perspective. What three or four things have you found to be essential to sustaining revival?

Seth Fawcet: First, we must adjust to the Spirit rather than making the Spirit adjust to us. This begins with those of us in leadership. For me, this includes a lot of praying in the Spirit. Where many come to church to get drunk in the Spirit, I plan to come to church to stay drunk. Romans chapter 12 declares that leaders are to lead diligently, and this starts in the spirit first. So, we have to learn to minister to our faith...love...hope...joy personally. As a leader, we must learn to feed faith and starve doubts...feed hope and starve fears...feed love and starve indifference...feed your joy. One of the ways I do this is to receive laying on of hands. In doing this, I am stirring up my own hunger. For me, this puts petrol in my tank. I also have to watch who I surround myself with. Separate yourself from negative people. I think that is easier for an apostle than a pastor because apostles' responses are instinctively different than pastors. They instinctively see the Kingdom, where the pastor instinctively sees the individual.

Following along with this, the leadership team of the church has to be totally committed for the long haul to revival. Leadership, especially upper tier, must practice personal revival. We lay hands on this group many times. Leaders should be the first to receive prayer - not the last! You cannot give what you do not have. You cannot lead where you are not going. In response to an accusation of being "yes men" an elder at Hope Centre said, "Of course, the Bible says we are to be likeminded." The voice of the people must never override the voice of the vision.

For us, this leads to the role of the apostolic and prophetic. That grace must be input into the church to sustain revival. They are the foundations. You see the default realm for these gifts is the Spirit, which is why they are so necessary to sustain revival.

Fourth, I would say don't milk the cow dry. Keep it fresh. Know when to transition. Michael, you will remember our discussions about stopping the 2000 meetings. That was a hard decision, but we knew it was the right decision. We did not milk the cow dry.

Michael Livengood: I also remember after 17 straight nights of services you and I talked about not exhausting the people. So, we adjusted the schedule.

Seth Fawcet: Let me put it this way. Preach them hungry don't preach them full.

Finally, in sustaining revival do not assume people understand what you are talking about. Those who join you on the journey do not understand the past, so we must bring them up to speed. We may not always tell the whole story, but we must help people understand who we are. Of course, people learn differently. Schools teach differently now, and we have to understand that. We need to know how different parts of the church learn, but we must keep putting the revival in context.

Keith Taylor: I know you asked for three or four, but let me mention five briefly. First, I think I have to talk about prayer. If prayer was essential in bringing it, it is essential in sustaining it. We are constantly seeking to keep a fresh prayer focus.

Second, I would also talk about the five-fold covering. Revival or Outpouring has been driven and maintained by recognizing and flowing with the five-fold ministries of the Holy Spirit.

Number three has been a heart for the lost. Cross Tabernacle has always been outward focused, and in revival, this has increased. A heart for the lost is a strong foundation stone for us.

Michael Livengood: Keith, please mention a few components of this outreach.

Keith Taylor: We are involved in compassion ministries to our city. This includes our major focus on single parents every December, but it is more. It includes our annual joy walk where we distribute bottles of Joy dishwashing detergent to poorer neighborhoods and pray with people. It involves our "ice cream" truck which gives away free popsicles in the same neighborhoods. It involves connecting with and releasing ministries to the felt needs. One of our staff leads this entire area of ministry. We also send out teams every week to witness and pray for people. This heart for the lost led us to support our local crisis pregnancy center and our local Teen Challenge center (drug rehabilitation program). Recently, we took around 40 people to participate in evangelistic and compassion ministry to one of our first people nations.

Michael Livengood: On a side note, I love the mix on your staff. You personally have native American blood in you. You have a staff member who is Iranian. Afro-American is a part of your leadership family. Forgive my interruption. What are the other two factors you wanted to mention?

Keith Taylor: I believe a city church vision is important for sustaining Outpouring. We pray with other leaders. Annually, we participate in a tent meeting led by another church. The area church expands our tents. I believe it is a book of Acts model.

Finally, I would mention five-fold relationships. The ministry of apostles, prophets and others have not only blessed the church, but relationships with other five-fold leaders creates accountability and integrity.

Graham Renouf: I tried to never lose sight of the big picture. Having been a part of an amazing church, that has seen many moves of God with an international impact and is just as hungry for God to do what He wants to do, I am learning the following.

I would suggest the challenge of learning how to flow where the Spirit is going. We need to be prepared to make adjustments. Leaders must be willing to be taught, to make changes. However, the changes must come from our heavenly Father's heart, so revival needs a constant revelation of the heart of the Father. Revival seems to always run the risk of complacency, so we have a challenge not to become complacent or take for granted the relationships God has given. Am I willing to adapt and make changes? Little foxes hinder where God wants to go.

Second, we must find a way for revival not to be one generation only. We want it to be intergenerational. I have watched some second-generation young people in revival saying, "I do not want to make the same sacrifices my parents made." My Initial response was anger toward that person. Then I felt the Holy Spirit tell me to take a deep breath and listen. When I did, I began to see what some second-generation church members saw. They saw broken families in some instances. They saw offspring of leaders probably burnt out and did not want that for their families. There is a danger in revival that we can turn the next generation off. I suspect some of my generation neglected some foundational things in our lives that would have made us more well-rounded and holistic, which would have helped those who have followed.

Finally, I think I would have to emphasize five-fold leadership in the churches. There is a grace that can come on five-fold leaders to allow others to move in the flow, and that is really important for sustaining a move of God.

Randall Burton: Knowing that you can sustain is important. Move away from the idea of revival as a gifted speaker. We need to understand revival culture can become a part of who you are, not just an extended meeting. The revival God sends you might be different than others, that is, it may look different. It may help you to know that historically revival was not viewed as a positive by everybody when it was happening.

For me, a second key issue is connections. It is important to be with the right people. These right people, other revival leaders, will help provide the right information you need for sustained revival.

For us, I think another key to sustain revival has been the understanding and recognition of what an intercessor is. An intercessor is more than a gifted prayer person. By the way, from my perspective, there is no such thing as a gift of intercession. While some may be called to intercede, all are called to pray. I began to handpick a team of intercessors. Our prayer room went from the crying room for the spiritually immature to a room where a powerful team pokes holes in heaven. I would handpick intercessors. They pray what the house prays. Not just the mantle. Not just people who are fascinated with the thought of being an intercessor, but rather people who are into the man. They are connected to the leader of the house. They are of the house. They carry the DNA of the house.

Tony Collis: You have to give up, to go up. When revival came in 2008, I gave up my preaching slot to you. When revival came, I gave up my respectability. When revival came, I gave up church agenda. When revival came, I gave up my own sensibilities. It is hard to look respectable from the floor or when you are as drunk in the Spirit as you can be and laughing hilariously.

In fact, I think every regressive step has been because either I or the church was not prepared to give something up. For example, revival comes, but it challenges our pride. For some in church, this can be a big struggle. Some are embarrassed by some of the things the Spirit does. So, they step back. For revival to sustain, you have to keep on giving things up. You give up what you know for what you do not know. You must hold everything with a wide-open hand.

Michael Livengood: Let's take one more look back before

157

we take a look into the future. If you had it all to do over again, what would you do differently now if anything? That is, of course, other than getting a better evangelist.

Seth Fawcet: The only major thing would be to adjust the Sunday morning service sooner. As a church, we were very hungry, but in the early days of revival, we did not do a great job of looking after the children. I probably would have worked more on making Sunday morning a family service rather than a revival service so as not to burn out our workers. I would watch over church life a bit closer. Watching over church life is important for sustaining the life of the church. The family service tends to build the congregation, while revival service tends to build the hunger. I would work on those ministries that help connect people to each other. We felt led to develop a cafe where people can share Sunday lunch. This has become very important for connecting people. I tell people our service on Sunday morning runs for three hours. The first 90 minutes is in the auditorium and the other 90 minutes in the cafe.

We want to develop a culture of honor which includes giving honor to other staff ministries. If I constantly allow the auditorium service to run too long (for personal glory time), I am not showing honor to our children workers, cafe workers and the like. We are members of one another.

This does not mean we shut down the move of the Holy Spirit on Sunday mornings. Congregations will recognize the genuine move of the Spirit. We are seeking to give the Spirit freedom to move, but operating within a basic time frame. The preacher is not the main thing. It is more important that people meet with God than that they heard a good sermon. Obviously, I do believe a good sermon can help people meet with God. However, I am struck by this thought. The children of Israel camped around the Presence of God while modern church camps around the sermon. The wind of John chapter three speaks of flexibility, so allow every service to feel different.

Keith Taylor: Ha, ha, ha! With all jokes aside, the evangelist actually is a very strong key that many times is overlooked. A strong, dedicated evangelist keeps the Great Commission at the forefront of all that is happening. This is nuts and bolts in Outpouring. Souls must be a priority to sustain it. At the same time, the five-fold evangelist flows in an Outpouring atmosphere differently than he flows in any other church setting. The five-fold evangelist is very "Glory aware." He follows and trusts the Holy Spirit to lead in totality, willing to be used by the Lord in an enlarged anointing. This includes allowing the personal packaging of a service to be forfeited, or better still yielded to the flow of the Holy Spirit for that service.

Graham Renouf: Hindsight is good, but I have a sneaky suspicion that God does not tell us everything about leading revival so that we will constantly be dependent upon Him. In other words, God will probably always leave us in the dark on some things.

I could go through a whole list like I would have done a better job of communication with the church. I would have paid more attention to the pastoral care of the church. I would have tried to be more aware of family needs, both in the church and in my own family. I would try to work more on bringing people with me and not driving them away.

But to be honest, my bottom line is I would not change anything. Even the mistakes we made were used by God to develop trust and other godly character. Faith relates to what we have not yet seen. There is an Old Book that we read that talks about leaning on God. Keep pressing in closer to God. That is what I always want to do better.

Randall Burton: The first would be to pay more attention to church life as the Outpouring unfolds. One of the tendencies is to blow off church life including Sunday school, youth, and other groups, but that is detrimental. The church life, discipleship and the like are extremely important. However, now we do them with revival DNA. I think I would have met more often with my leaders early on. I would take them with me to stuff I was going to.

Michael Livengood: Who would these leaders have been?

Randall Burton: Oh, you know, staff, elders, key people, anybody who pushes a mop or carries a microphone needs to go to revival. Do not assume your DNA is in them. You have to develop it in them. People will come in who do not have your DNA, so it must be developed in them. Take people with you! Sometimes the journey is as important as the destination. If your people go to revivals and so forth with you, they will realize you are not just on vacation.

Tony Collis: Unfortunately for us, the issue of revival became the two camps. Some were pro-revival, and others were anti-revival. In hindsight, I would try to talk to the leaders of the second camp on a pastoral level, to seek to provide personal encouragement and talk challenges through with them. I did do that, but in hindsight, I would have started earlier. We may have been able to hold off some of the issues. Hoping they would get on board was not enough. I should have engaged them before we lost them from revival. On the positive side of this issue, it increased my humility and personal growth.

This one may be very subjective, but in hindsight, I should have delayed the family holiday that we took in the middle of those nineteen weeks. The holiday was important, but I feel I lost some connection with what God was doing and with the momentum of revival. I was prepared to give up the church agenda and those kinds of things. Now, I think it would have been good to have delayed the holiday. My family would have accepted it.

I definitely should have taken more time to rest during the revival. Revival can be physically demanding, and I should have rested more.

I would place more value on prayer. I could have given some church stuff to others so that I could have protected the place of prayer. I believe the leader of the house can protect that place more than any person can. I would give up other stuff to protect the value of prayer.

I also found I would have approached differently the challenge between local and national ministry, the balance between personal ministry and the local church. A national ministry is opening up to me, but I am finding I would rather spend time in the prayer room.

Michael Livengood: I believe your thoughts and experiences will help others who are in the white waters of revival. Let's move on to looking into the future. What is your heart or vision for future revival?

Seth Fawcet: City-wide transformation! Our responsibility is to take responsibility for the Presence of God in our city. Write it into the fabric of your church. The DNA of Hope Centre is to spread revival as a church to the nation and nations. I do not have a separate ministry name because I want Hope Centre to send me. We believe Hope Centre's mandate is to stir up revival. Our oldies (senior citizens group) love feeling like they are touching Germany. I travel as a part of Hope Centre.

Keith Taylor: I know I can't go back to the times prior to Outpouring. My heart is to pursue His Glory as He leads. I have seen the Holy Spirit through the years adjust the services constantly, changing the comfort zones of His moving. I want to stay in His flow, which simply means being in a constant state of His leadership. That, my friend, always involves sea and river crossings. My heart is to go out stronger than when I stepped in.

Outpouring has become, I believe, the calling the Lord placed me in many years ago at a kitchen table. I find it amusing now that I was an instrument of praise and writing songs; interesting that from that point on I became a driven man for the Presence of the Lord the rest of my days. From that kitchen table visitation, my life has been a constant drive toward His Presence.

Graham Renouf: God's heart is that no one should perish. I just want to be a part of what I believe I have seen in the spirit that God is going to do in the States and New Zealand. I believe the greatest outpourings are yet to come. I want to be positioned for the wave that is coming, so I must get closer to Him. I want to be actively doing what the Father is doing. I believe the five-fold is going to be huge for the future.

Randall Burton: Well, beyond leading a healthy, growing church with a revival culture I want to see my city enmeshed in revival. I believe the heart of the Father is for His Kingdom. When I wrote the book, River Rising, I wrote there is a difference between a river flowing and a river that has gone outside the banks into the community. That is what I want to see. Ecclesiastes 1:7 says "All rivers run into the sea." Revival is all about that. I want to see an impact on the nation. This Outpouring/Revival must go into the sea.

Tony Collis: I don't ever want to stop believing for an even greater revival. I am wide open to that. I want to make room for it at the slightest whiff. I intend to embrace the ugly with the beautiful. I understand ugly will happen, but I will focus on the beauty. It is in my heart to see my family engaged in revival even as I want to try to protect them from the ugly part. I accept that revival will forever define me. The year 2000 changed me forever, but 2008 was that ten times over!

Michael Livengood: It would be interesting to explore some of those remarks a bit more, but let's wrap up this discussion with one more question. What would be the three or four things that are at the top of your list that a pastor in revival needs to understand?

Seth Fawcet: Number one is your church leadership has to be totally committed to a new reality, a restoration to normality. Number two, recognize the need for five-fold ministry influence in your local church. Number three, understand that whatever it takes to get a move of God will be required to sustain a move of God. Watch distractions.

Finally, every human being has two instincts. One is to breathe, and the other is to drink. Breathing brings life, but drinking sustains life. Solid food given too soon will kill a baby, so the Bible says drink more than eat. Too many moves of God kill the baby because they give the baby solid food too soon.

Keith Taylor: Revival will not be sustained without prayer.

This is both personal and corporate. Number two, revival will only be sustained by passion. This is a passion for souls, a passion for His Word, a passion for praise and worship. Number three, Outpouring is all about Presence. To sustain this Presence involves changing the atmosphere and the culture of your church and then your city. Last, a five-fold leadership model is essential. This includes covering, relationships, and accountability.

Graham Renouf: Your personal relationship with God must be maintained. Make it the primary thing to seek His face without compromise - no going back. Give Him room to move. I would encourage you to trust the God that is in you.

Resist the temptation to lower the standard to where the people are, but rather bring them up to where you are. Pastoring by default is about people, but revival is about Him. Don't pander to the soul, but keep the focus on the spirit.

As you seek to keep hunger levels maintained, remember to lead rather than push the people. Bring the people with you. There are exceptions. You cannot please all the people, so do not become a people pleaser rather than a God pleaser.

Randall Burton: I think I would want to say, first of all, it really is not about you!

Don't assume anything. Don't assume your church is on board…or your city…or your friends.

Realize this is a process, not an event or season. It is a lifestyle lived out through a leader who is sold out for God, who does not have any recourse except to go forward. Realize there is nothing to go back to. You have to live it…sleep it…eat it. Do not allow Pharisees to keep you from doing that.

You must pastor people and work with pastors whose people want to go with you and want to change churches. You are uncompromisingly going after revival.

.

12

CAN YOU GROW A CHURCH AND HAVE REVIVAL?

Is it possible to pastor a church in revival and see the church grow numerically at the same time? I think pastors ask me this question more than any other. The author of a recent book, who serves as an executive officer within his denomination and has a portfolio including credentialing of ministers, responds to the same question. During the process of credentialing, he asks the questioner about their views of the person and ministry of the Holy Spirit. The question seems to produce discomfort. These young Pentecostal leaders often admit they struggle over how to answer. They want to see the Holy Spirit move, but they do not want to pastor a church that is irrelevant.

From the years I have spent in pastoral ministry, my library is full of books on church growth. Both churches I pastored experienced a significant numerical increase in a season of no growth for most others. During my early years of itinerant ministry, I sought to observe what caused churches to grow, always anticipating that someday I might be a senior leader of a church again. While that has not been the plan of God for my life, I remain interested in the things that cause the Kingdom of God to grow.

The Wow Factor

By this point, you realize that I am uncompromisingly a revivalist …river person…outpouring oriented. At the same time, I recognize many believe a church cannot be large and growing while being Pentecostal in style and beliefs.

I simply disagree with them.

I do so on the basis that the largest churches in the world are usually Pentecostal or charismatic in theology and practice. I do acknowledge the largest ones in the United States are usually considered evangelical, and even those that are Pentecostal in doctrine are often not Pentecostal in practice.

Another reason I disagree is based on personal experience. I have watched the Pentecostal church world for many years, and I do recognize many of those churches are shrinking. However, I currently work with three revival churches that are experiencing or have experienced significant growth numerically. Actually, the number is larger. Only two days before this writing, I spoke with my mother who has served as an interim at a church for the last two years. In that season the church has nearly doubled in attendance.

The material I present in this chapter will not be exhaustive nor complete because that would take a book on church growth itself, but I want to observe a few things these growing revival churches seem to have in common.

First, they are committed to growing the Kingdom of God, and they are not ashamed to desire numerical increase. This is not a desire for numbers for the sake of numbers alone, but a recognition that numbers represent people, and they are committed to populating heaven. The missions statement of one of those churches includes a line about becoming a large congregation. Outreach is important to them. From raw evangelistic events to more subtle pre-evangelism activities that serve their communities, they have consistently turned their attention outward.

Secondly, these churches are led by visionary, some would say, apostolic leaders. These are strong leaders, but they are not dictatorial nor tyrannical. I understand there are different models of church life. Some feel very strongly about a plurality of leaders. They are an elder driven model. Some churches feel very strongly about being democratic. They are congregational driven. Some churches feel strongly about being an extension of a denomination or stream. Their approach toward ministry and church life is determined by patterns within that denomination. Please do not hear this last statement as a condemnation of denominations. I am credentialed with the world's largest Pentecostal denomination.

My personal experience, though, is that rarely do the models I have mentioned experience ongoing significant growth. Where large churches practicing the above leadership models do exist, I would suggest the following. Their growth probably came during an earlier period of church life under a strong apostolic type of leader, or the growth probably came during a time in society when church involvement was more the norm. I am just not aware of any significant church growth that takes place apart from a strong apostolic type of leader. The style of the church may run from "seeker" to "purpose-driven" to "traditional" to "revival", but growing churches are led by strong leaders. Surveys support my personal experience. The senior pastor plays a key role in growing churches.

There is a temptation on the part of "river" or "revival" type churches to discount the role of leadership. One pastor said to me, "If my stream does one more conference on leadership I will cram it down their throat." Let me be very clear on this. I do not believe leadership can replace the Presence and the anointing, but without leadership, revival itself will not produce strong growing churches.

Revival reveals what already exists. Revival will reveal any cracks in the leadership. It will expose any shaky foundations. Revival itself does not make leadership strong. If you were a poor leader before the revival, the revival itself would not make you a good leader. Therefore, I would suggest the leader who is pursuing the Presence of God and revival needs to also develop his or her leadership skills.

The Wow Factor

The strong revival leader is surrounded by leaders of similar spirit and vision. Moses had an Aaron. As a pastor, I was highly motivated by a story from one of the great churches of my denomination. About half of the pastoral staff, including the senior pastor, and about half of the board of deacons were killed in a tragic plane accident. They were returning from a mission trip when their small plane went down. As the state superintendent of my denomination met with the surviving board members, they asked if he would help them find a new pastor. He assured them he would. Then they shared the strangest statement he had heard from a church board. "When you find a pastor, please tell him we are 'yes men.'" He asked them to explain this statement. He had never had a church board tell him they were "yes men." They said, "We were a very average church for many years until we came to understand that God could speak to our pastor. We are not threatened by that. Our job is to help him carry out the vision God has given him." That spirit caused the church to become one of the largest churches in the state.

Everything we saw happen in our last pastorate came because the leadership of the church (deacon board) believed in and adopted my vision. We did not spend time squabbling over direction. Rather, time was spent developing that direction.

The spirit of this is seen in Joshua 1:16, *"So they answered Joshua, saying, 'All that you command us we will do, and wherever you send us we will go. Just as we heeded Moses in all things, so we will heed you. Only the Lord, your God, be with you, as He was with Moses. Whoever rebels against your command and does not heed your words, in all that you command him, shall be put to death. Only be strong and of good courage"* (NKJV).

In my imagination, I can see the note sent from the elders and deacons being handed to a pastor by an usher. "Dear pastor, please be aware that Sister Snuffleuptogus was complaining and murmuring against you and the direction of the church. Do not fear. We took her outside and stoned her to death. Be strong and lead us on."

Can You Grow a Church and Have Revival?

Ok, I'm <u>not</u> encouraging the stoning to death of dissenters, but making the point that strong churches have leaders who surround the leader. They encourage him or her to be everything God has called them to be. They help bring to pass the vision God has for that church. These leaders can make or break revival.

Several years ago, I was preaching a revival in a northern state of the USA. These were good people, albeit a bit conservative by background. Things were definitely happening outside of their box! I went to pray for a lady one night and was strongly checked by the Holy Spirit. I was to pray, but I was not to touch her. My hand was only a few inches away from her head, so she likely knew I was there, but I did not touch her. Her husband stood next to her watching me as I prayed and as she fell to the floor under the power of God. I did not feel I was to pray for him, so I did not. The next night she was at the altar, and once again he was standing next to her with eyes open. I did not touch her. From a distance of at least four or five feet, I pointed at her. I am sure she did not know I was there. Once again, she hit the floor. The third night I was probably fifteen feet away from her. Again, her eyes were closed. Again, he was watching me. I felt just to wave in her direction. Again, she fell to the floor. He walked up to me and said, "Pray for me." I did, and nothing appeared to happen.

Sunday morning this same man was leading the worship. He acknowledged things happening in the revival that he did not understand and that many questions existed in the minds of the people. However, the combination of the change in his wife's life and the fact he knew I had not pushed her convinced him God was in it. He told the people, "I do not understand it all, but I want to be a bridge to help you across. I know God is in this." The pastor turned to me and said, "That statement is huge. You will never realize how huge it is." As this leader embraced what God was doing it encouraged others to take the same step. Leaders need leaders to stand with them.

The fourth principle revival churches experiencing church

169

growth follow is that they recognize roadblocks and are willing to deal with them. They live as did the men of Issachar, who, according to 1Chronicles 12:32 *"understood the times and knew what Israel should do."*

Revival leaders need to understand the times. They must understand the culture they live in and even more so hear from God as to what they should do.

There are keys to every situation. Not every key fits every lock, but every lock has a specific key. Church growth revival leaders find the key that unlocks their city in God.

My father drilled this little cliché into me, *"We are anchored to the rock and geared to the times."*

We must understand those things that are immovable and those things that should be moved. There is a difference between fads and principles. Fads will always change, but principles never will. Fads are often short-lived vehicles used to carry out a principle, but a ministry built on fads will not endure.

A perfect illustration of this is the church cafe. Fifteen to twenty years ago very few churches had cafes. In fact, some denominations would have preached against it. Today, most churches I minister in have some type of cafe or coffee bar. It may consist of a few tables in the lobby, or it may be a full-blown cafe with a kitchen that rivals any commercial enterprise, but many have some area designated for this purpose.

For some, the church cafe was a fad. Churches joined in the trend toward the café because everyone else was doing it, and they did not want to appear out of touch. For some, the café posed problems. They thought it would produce quick growth. It didn't. Others saw the cafe as a means to develop relationships (fellowship) in the church and as an opportunity for leadership to connect with people. A lot of pastoral work can be accomplished in a relatively short period in the cafe after service. Often the cafe has faltered for the first two examples but succeeded well with the third. I know of at least one church that has used proceeds from a cafe to fund much of the mission outreach from the church. The principle was fellowship or pastoral connection. The method employed was a church cafe. The *rock* is fellowship. The timely *gear* is the cafe.

Growing revival churches recognize roadblocks to church growth and are not afraid of sacrificing sacred cows. Some methods that were awesome fifty years ago are counterproductive today. The constant challenge is to recognize the difference between fad and principle.

In the early days of revival, the Lord spoke to me about learning to live by principles. Worship is a principle. Singing is a Biblical way to carry out this mandate. However, the style of song is more a matter of taste and culture.

Again, I acknowledge I am unapologetically a revival junkie. I have friends who have spent much time attacking the "seeker friendly" type of churches. I have been guilty of doing the same. I must admit, I do have issues with anyone compromising core Biblical doctrines and practices. Salvation by the blood of Jesus is non-negotiable. The Baptism in the Holy Spirit is the same for me. Healing was not intended to be divisive but to be a blessing. I will not compromise these things. However, there are many things I can learn from the "seeker" style of church.

For example, does my language make sense to the unchurched or do only the initiated understand me? This message was brought home to me while giving a salvation invitation several years ago. I was inviting people who wanted to give their lives to Jesus to come to the altar. Standing in the balcony was a young man who had never been to a revival service before. His religious background was Catholic. The message had made sense, and he wanted to respond to it. However, the word "altar" was throwing him off. He could see nothing at the front of that Assemblies of God church that looked like the altar of his church. Fortunately, the school teacher standing next to him recognized his dilemma and brought him to the front of the building. Later that night when she shared with me what had happened I made a significant change. From that night, I invite those who are asking Jesus into their lives to "leave your seat, make your way to the nearest aisle, walk to the front of this building, stand in this open space here at the front and face me." Everybody understands that direction. Later I may explain why we call the front of this building the altar. Once I have them standing at the front, I bring up the prayer team. I lead them in a sinner's prayer and have the prayer team (altar counselors) also pray and counsel them.

Does my church make the visitor feel welcome? What is their experience like from the time they enter the parking lot to the contact with people after the meeting? As a pastor, I was aware people go to church to meet God and to make a friend, but not necessarily in that order. I could pretty much guarantee they would meet God because I would pray that through. However, I needed help if the visitors were going to meet and make a friend. Revival does not change those realities. I once pastored the oldest, most historic Pentecostal church in a community of 10,000. I think there were five other Pentecostal churches in my community. At least four of them traced their roots to my church. I was told at least three of the evangelical churches did the same. We probably had the best facilities. I thought we had the best preaching (OK, I am a little biased on that). Our music team was better than others. However, the reality was that at least two of those churches were growing faster than mine. The church nursery is just as important to most people as the platform performance of your pastor.

The Presence of the Lord God has found your church, but can the people find it? Are directions to the church restroom clear, or does the visitor need a seeing eye dog to find it? The greeters are among the most important people you have. They are the frontline.

Being an itinerant preacher can be an interesting experience. For many years we traveled by RV. Usually, it was placed behind the church in the car park. In those days, I often went into the church building early to pray, leaving my wife to enter the building on her own later. Since she was unknown by the greeter at the door, her experience more typically represented what the average visitor

172

could expect. On far too many occasions her experience was the kind that discouraged people. Often people make up their minds about the church before the first song is sung.

Here is a personal gripe. I hate a service that takes up twenty minutes of time for everyone to greet everyone else. I dislike that for two reasons. First, I must keep extending myself. I have to stretch my comfort zones. If I, as a professional, struggle with twenty minutes of talking to people I don't know, what is going through the heart of someone who has never been to church before, or someone who is a bit shy? My second gripe is very personal. As a guest speaker, I normally have a very limited time frame to preach on a Sunday morning and those twenty minutes are like gold to me.

Principle number five relates to prayer. In the growing revival church, prayer is given more than lip service. You can grow large numbers through your program, activities, and promotion. Apparently, you can even do that without prayer. However most, if not all, of the dynamically alive and growing congregations I am connected with recognize the importance of prayer. First, the leaders themselves pray. Secondly, they find creative ways to keep the people engaged in prayer.

Principle number six has to do with the purpose of the church. In a growing revival church, the DNA, or the purpose of the church, is clearly understood. In years gone by some called this the mission statement. I attempted to make this something clearly understood by the church I pastored. For those years we operated on the WIFE'S principle:

Worship
Instruction
Fellowship
Evangelism
Service

Today, I would say, "We exist to make disciples, and we will do that through worship, instruction, fellowship, evangelism, and service."

All the above can and should take place within the context of revival. I will argue that the revival described in the book of Acts was to be the normal pattern of church life and church growth. Methods will change, but those five principles do not. They are Biblical.

The final principle is perhaps the heart of the issue. How do you make the unchurched comfortable with a revival/river/Outpouring atmosphere? Some think you must downplay the activity of the Holy Spirit as if to suggest He does not understand human nature. As I listen to some, I begin to pick up the sense they feel a need to protect their people from the Holy Spirit. First, may I suggest your people do not need to be protected from Him. Secondly, they are His people, not yours! The spinoff of this philosophy suggests we need to place, I started to say hide, all Holy Spirit activities in another room or another service.

Let me suggest two alternatives. Celebrate it! If you are comfortable and natural with the work of the Holy Spirit others will be comfortable as well. Many unchurched people do not know what is proper decorum in church anyway. My experience suggests it is usually the religious, not the unchurched, who are uncomfortable with the activity of the Spirit.

More importantly, explain it. It is okay to take time to explain what the Holy Spirit is doing. You can do this privately to your guests. If you suspect they may see something in your church they are unfamiliar with, why not make a pre-emptive strike? Share in advance what they can expect. If that is not workable, you can take time after a service to chat with your friends. Ask them what was different about your church in light of their previous experiences? Then be prepared to give them a Biblical explanation for what took place. It is alright to admit you do not know an answer but will find it.

As a pastor, you can do this publicly from the pulpit. When I was in pastoral ministry, I often explained the vocal gifts of the Holy Spirit; tongues, interpretation, prophecy, after they occurred. I would say something to the effect "the Bible teaches that God not only speaks to us through His Word, but He will also speak to us through what the Bible calls gifts from His Spirit." I would explain what just happened can be found in 1 Corinthians chapters 12 and 14. In the space of two or three minutes or less, I could explain what just happened. Not only did I give the people an understanding of a Biblical experience, but I also created a sense of safety. I have done this in reference to manifestations as well. One career missionary observed the strength of the revival service he attended was the three to five-minute spot where the pastor or I explained things like people falling down during service. He felt safe.

Let me close this chapter by suggesting you cannot lead where you have not been yourself. You want a church that is both experiencing strong numerical increase and a strong flow of the Spirit (revival). It can happen. There is no need to sacrifice one to get the other. Yes, leadership will be required. Perhaps that is why God put you there.

13

THE AFTERMATH:
WHEN BAD THINGS HAPPEN TO A GOOD REVIVAL

Some live under the false assumption that real revival will never have any issues connected to it. A friend of mine who was a quality pastor with a good record and who served on the state-wide board of his denomination experienced a significant revival in his church and city. Among the scores of people who came to salvation was a man involved with the mafia. The first time he came to the revival he stepped into the lobby and then ran from the meeting, spinning the tires on his pickup as he attempted to flee the Presence of God. However, that Presence drew him back again the next night. As he stepped into the church lobby, he was confronted by a Presence of God that put him on the floor. Even before the service began this man with mafia connections crawled from the lobby to the altar area of the building to get right with God.

Yet seventeen weeks into that outpouring the pastor received a petition calling for a business meeting to vote out the evangelist. Not long after they called for his departure as well. Because of these actions the denominational board felt the revival had not been genuine.

The Wow Factor

Some pastors and church leaders allow issues whether perceived or real to keep them from entering a move of God. A church located in the deep southern part of the United States asked its pastor to leave because of revival. I was invited by his successor to come and minister at the church. I went to preach out of curiosity. I wanted to learn whether my friend had made mistakes in leading that revival, or if indeed the people truly did not want a move of God. It soon became clear to me the people did not want revival.

My experience during the four days of the scheduled meeting was unique. I can only describe it by saying each night the Holy Spirit would come after the crowd left the building. It was so pronounced that the pastor began pleading with his church to linger longer because God was showing up just after they left. However, they did not do so, and the Holy Spirit was not inclined to reveal Himself while they were there.

The Pastor told Linda the revival was about him and his past. As a teen, the church he attended experienced a revival. Tragically, what began well turned sour. As a result, he grew paranoid over revival. He recognized the revival they were experiencing was God asking him if he was willing to move beyond his past and allow revival to come to his church.

I do not want you to be afraid of a real move of God. I believe REVIVAL IS WORTH ANY PRICE REQUIRED.

In this chapter, we will look at a Biblical passage that describes the aftermath of revival. Then I will share stories of the bad and the ugly of revivals I have experienced. The purpose will be to prepare you emotionally for the types of things you may encounter. I want you to know you are not alone, and I do not want you blindsided. However, I do not intend to leave you feeling helpless. I want to help prepare you with some suggestions for dealing with some of the issues of revival.

The Story of Elijah

Scripture reveals that revival brings issues. 1 Kings chapters 17-19 tell the story of the events preceding, during and following major revival. In this revival, the entire nation repented of sin. Miracles accompanied the ministry of Elijah.

Please understand, revival creates opposition. In the text Jezebel, the pagan queen was stirred up. Some opposition is from our human flesh, while other opposition is demonic in origin. Ahab returns to Jezreel from the outpouring of the Spirit on the mountain…he has seen the fire consume the sacrifice…he has seen the people fall on their faces in repentance…he has probably been drenched by the rain as it fell on him as he was coming back to Jezreel. Yet, with all of that he has not been changed.

He does not come back and say to his wife Jezebel, "Jezzie, it is time for you and me to repent…to get things right with God." Ahab is like some people who seem to see everything and yet miss everything. They fail to grasp the message behind the manifestations. No, Ahab comes back and reports "all that Elijah had done." In one sense, I suppose that is human nature. Ahab only seemed to notice the human element. He failed to understand the fire that consumed the sacrifice had not been started by Elijah. The rain that fell from darkened clouds had not come from Elijah. These were God events! He should have said, "Jezzie, let me tell you what God did up there on that mountain!"

Jezebel responds to the information that the prophets of Baal have been put to death with the sword by sending a message to Elijah. It was not a message indicating a realization that God had come into the camp. It was not a message asking, "What must I do to get right with God?" Instead, she tells Elijah she plans on killing him. She should have walked in repentance, but instead, revenge came into her heart.

Your revival will not cause Satan to flee your city. Often revival simply stirs up Jezebel.

Secondly, revival will not remove your humanity. James 5:17-18 puts it this way, *"Elias was a man subject to like passions as we are, and he prayed earnestly that it might not rain: and it rained not on the earth by the space of three years and six months. And he prayed again, and the heaven gave rain, and the earth brought forth her fruit."*

Elijah experienced the same passions as we do. He felt the same things we feel. He experienced fear. In 1 Kings 19:3 he runs for his life. Some scholars believe since Satan could not stop the revival, he plotted to take Elijah out of it and thereby limit its effectiveness. This appeared to be what happened. Perhaps Elijah was caught off guard by the ferocity of Jezebel's attack. He may have been a bit over-confident because of the great victory God had given him.

Elijah became isolated. He left his servant behind, perhaps expressing a desire to escape. Scholars are divided, but it is at least possible Elijah left his "armorbearer." I have watched Satan seek to isolate revivalists. He understands they are easier to pick off that way. Denominational or church opposition, real, or perceived, contributes to this tendency. Elijah experienced depression. In fact, he prayed to die. Please understand that revival will not make you immune to any of these problems. Do not be surprised when fear … flight … escapism or depression surface. Just do not give in to them.

The good news is God's Spirit nurtures revival. In 1 Kings 19:5-7 angels ministered to Elijah. Let me encourage revivalists by saying, "You too will be ministered to by angels, whether you see them or not." God supernaturally sustained Elijah. We read how God provided rest and food. God baked him a cake. God knows what you need, and He will supply it to you. Sometimes in revival, you need to pull back and rest in the Lord. It is not unspiritual to have physical needs met such as food and rest. Then God prepared a supernatural encounter for Elijah, at which time he received a new assignment.

The Not So Good…the Bad…and the Ugly of Revival

I love to tell the stories of what the Lord does in revival. One prophetic word indicated I had become famous for the stories. Then it went on to say there was a revival coming, the stories of which I would not be able to keep up with. However, not every story of revival is one of glory. Some are not so good. Some are bad. Some are downright ugly.

I am going to share some of the challenges we have seen surface in revival. I am going to do that to help you understand how Satan and human flesh will resist moves of God.

Even during revival war can break out over the music. Music is such a vital part of our worship of the Lord that we should not be surprised Satan would choose to fight it so hard. Many pastors have discovered that revival can lead to a two-camp church. For one pastor the two camps centered around the music and the manifestations of the Holy Spirit. He attempted to resolve the situation by starting a second service. The early service sang more traditional hymns and did not expect any "out of the box" moments. The second service sang the more contemporary revival types of songs and every service had a full-on expectation. I commend the pastor for his willingness to look for a solution, but the plan was only partially successful. He discovered there were some in the first service who were embarrassed over what was happening in the second service and did not want any revival manifestations to happen in their church. Period.

In another church, the word of knowledge regarding sin and the accompanying call to repentance created such opposition that it led to the closure of a revival.

In another church, one woman was extremely upset over her perceived loss of position and ministry due to extended meetings. The extended meetings had brought a temporary shut-down of other events to focus on responding to the Holy Spirit. She began pressuring her pastor over when her private kingdom could start again. There will always be the challenge of creating space for God to move in revival and determining which ministries are to be restored and when this is to happen.

Sometimes revival creates interesting but perhaps not so edifying conversations or incidents. In one of those, I was making my way from the rear of an auditorium to the front, shaking hands with people as I went. One man pointedly refused to shake my hand and told me he had come to rebuke me in the Lord, and he called me a charlatan. On another occasion, a young gang banger told the person who had brought him to the meeting he wanted to punch me. In yet another service a lady attempted to karate kick me while I was praying for her. A different tactic was displayed by the man who "wanted to put me in his hip pocket." Later he called the religious press to stir up problems. I can think of two men in different cities who would come to the weekly revival prayer meeting and then pointedly refuse to participate. Their very presence created a shadow on the prayer meeting.

I was the evangelist for a seven-week revival in a northern state. During those seven weeks, we saw 300 people commit their lives to Jesus Christ. However, for many people that revival was controversial because people falling to the ground was a part of those meetings. These manifestations invoked memories in the minds of some of a period in their church history when the city had rejected and persecuted them. They were afraid they were going to find themselves repeating that cycle. One individual told the pastor, "It took us 30 years to live down this reputation, and we do not want it again."

Revival may also bring personal rejection. For twelve years I was not allowed to preach at what was my home church. My pastor who was a friend, a board member, and a good man was afraid of revival, therefore he would not allow me to preach in the church. I am reasonably certain I had some meetings canceled because I was seen to be a part of "that Brownsville thing." I will hasten to say I also had other doors open to me for the same reason. Rejection is not pleasant, but sometimes it is a part of the price of going after revival.

The pastor of one revival church has on more than one occasion had his integrity questioned. He was even accused of manufacturing revival! Division has occurred within the larger family. Some have challenged the physical reactions this pastor experiences when the manifest Presence of God comes upon him. He often has difficulty standing or even speaking. In personal conversation, he told me that these sometimes make him feel foolish, but he is willing to be a fool for Christ if the Lord asks that of him. A former national leader of my denomination, during a time of national exposure of our movement because of the moral failures of certain high-profile preachers, told a group of evangelists, "Being misunderstood is the price of leadership."

Pastors are often stunned when those they thought would embrace revival do not. On the other hand, they are often pleasantly surprised when those they did not think would embrace revival do. Criticism is a major tool of the devil to fight you and revival. During one of the most significant revivals I have ever preached, the wife of a nearby pastor began to criticize us, based upon misconceptions she picked up from people in their church who attended the revival.

In another very significant revival, we became aware of criticism from the pulpit of a neighboring pastor who had never been to the revival. Though he had not attended the revival, he announced to his church that it was not a revival at all. During a denominational event held at the church where the revival occurred, it was clear his people would not associate with people from the revival. A variation of this attitude was the church who drove hundreds of miles to attend a nationally known revival but would not cross town to attend the revival that had broken out in their midst.

Some Simple Suggestions

Not everyone will embrace revival, but are there things you can do to decrease the fall out of revival? Absolutely. Here are some suggestions to help resolve these and other similar situations.

Probably one of the most important things you can do is teach a lot. Where it is possible, I attempt to explain what God seems to be doing. This teaching often requires a focus on manifestations. My first self-published booklet came about as a direct result of attempting to answer the questions of honest seekers and the objections of the critics. The latter needed to be done to help the former. Teaching not only helps the open, honest questioner (even skeptic) to understand, but it gives a sense of security to people who need to know someone up there is in charge and knows what is going on. A little study of Scripture and church history was very helpful for me. Teaching does not have to require 30-minute blocks of time. I have found a lot can be accomplished in three to five-minute segments in a service.

My second suggestion is to turn down the rhetoric. Let's not create unnecessary enemies. Evangelists can be somewhat notorious for creating straw enemies they then have to knock over. Try to avoid the "us versus them" mentality of revival. In an earlier chapter, you read of the two-camp syndrome. Tragically, we as leaders have sometimes added to this issue by the way we approach revival. Indeed, some approach church life from this vantage point. Not everyone who disagrees is my enemy. Sometimes we create mountains of things that should have remained small hills.

Thirdly, I would suggest you try to provide as many options as possible as did the church I mentioned above. Sometimes that will work. Sometimes it will not. I would suggest it is important to pick your battles in revival.

Choosing to pick your battles in revival leads to an awareness you will ignore some things. Some things are linked to revival itself, and some things are simply an aggravated part of church life.

The Aftermath-When Bad Things Happen to a Good Revival

Remember that everything intensifies in revival. Some things do not need to be dignified with a response, but others must always receive one. I will always seek to give time to the honest enquirer. I am willing to dialogue with those who disagree with me if I sense they are seekers of truth. However, in the philosophy of Nehemiah, I am not prepared to come down from building this wall to just debate with you.

In my book "The Glory Factor" published by Evergreen Press, I devote an entire chapter to the things successful revival leaders do well. One of these is: Do not be afraid to lead. Nature abhors a vacuum. If you don't lead someone else will. If you are a pastor, I want you to believe God knew revival was going to come when He placed you in that church. Now, He is going to help you.

Since many of the controversial issues tend to center around what happens when people are prayed for, be careful how you pray. If possible, heavy hands should be avoided. I work hard not to appear to push. This means be careful how you position your hands. During one revival a youth pastor appeared to be pushing people to the floor. I finally took him under my wing and let him walk with me as I was praying for people. I was very lightly touching people under their elbows. The power of God came, and many fell, but it did not appear I was pushing them. When God is in it, He does not need your help. You will need to decide about catchers. In most instances, I recommend catchers be available. They can be a protection for the novice believer who feels required to fall, or for the over-energetic prayer team member who thinks God needs his assistance, or for the person sitting in their seat wondering if it is safe to receive prayer. They can also protect you from an unfortunate lawsuit.

While I am on the thought of the catchers, I would suggest training sessions be held for prayer team members and catchers. We should not assume everyone knows how to minister at the altar. I have included in the appendix some guidelines for prayer team members and catchers. These guidelines were borrowed from some

185

guidelines I saw followed at an annual conference in New Zealand.

We want the altar to be a safe place. We want it to be a place where people encounter the God who loves them. We want it to be the place where people encounter the God who is so strong and powerful that a holy fear is also generated. However, I also recognize our prayer teams are made up of people. Give people time to grow. Ministry teams will need time to grow. Those being ministered to need time to grow too.

I encourage you to stay based on solid Pentecostal, Biblical foundations and then just let the wind blow. I try never to forget that I am not required to be loved by everyone. I prefer to be accepted by everyone. However, at the end of this life, I will have only one Judge who matters. Therefore, I am committed to pleasing Him.

While this may not appear spiritual, it is very important that you maintain a sense of humor. Learn to laugh at yourself. A sense of humor can defuse a lot of tough situations. Stay balanced. That may mean going golfing now and then!

Focus on the blessings of the revival. I can focus on the critics. I can focus on the cringe factor stuff, or I can focus on the blessing and what God is doing!

One of the wisest things God helped me to do was to develop a mentor. Actually, I cannot take credit. God in His great mercy and compassion on me and those I was going to minister to, gave me a relationship with the senior associate pastor of the Brownsville revival. Carey Robertson became my "go-to guy." When I had questions, which was often, I called him. Not only did I form a relationship with him, but I also formed relationships with other revival junkies. Don't be afraid of people God places in your life to help you. You may not follow all their counsel, but these relationships will protect you and the Kingdom of God.

Finally, WELCOME TO REVIVAL! Recognize some stuff is going to happen. You are going to grow. God will not fall off His throne.

APPENDIX ONE

Signs and Wonders in the Book of Acts

1) While it does not use the phrase "sign and wonders" Acts 1:3 says Jesus showed Himself to His disciples after His death and resurrection "by many infallible proofs, being seen of them forty days."

2) In Acts 1:9 Jesus ascends into heaven in the plain sight of His followers.

3) In Acts 2:11 we find the church speaking in tongues in the language of the hearers. This had been preceded by the sound of a wind and tongues of fire.

4) Nameless signs and wonders were done by the apostles (Acts 2:43).

5) The healing of a lame man in Acts 3:1-11.

6) A house was shaken (Acts 4:31) which also says they were filled with the Holy Spirit, boldness, great power, and great grace. The followers of Jesus had prayed for boldness to speak the Word and for the Lord to grant healings and signs and wonders in the Name of Jesus.

7) Ananias and Sapphira fell dead. (Acts 5:5-10).

8) Signs and wonders included healing by Peter's shadow and people who were vexed with unclean spirits being healed. (Acts 5:12-17).

9)   The apostles were delivered from prison by angels. (Acts 5:18-19).

10) Stephen the deacon, full of faith and power, does great wonders and miracles among the people (Acts 6:8). The word for faith is "pistis." It appears 244 times and is translated faith 239 of those times in the KJV. It includes the thought of conviction of the truth of something. Stephen is also said to be full of power. The word is "dunamis." It seems to me the thought is that Stephen did these great wonders and miracles because of the combination of faith and anointing. Virtue was flowing, and he was operating at a level of faith for it to happen. It is possible for both to occur. The phrase "wonders and miracles" is elsewhere translated signs and wonders.

11) Philip, the evangelist, preaches in Samaria, and they see great signs and wonders occur. Demoniacs were delivered, and the sick were healed. Particular notice is given that the lame began to walk and those with palsy were healed (Acts 8:5-7).

12) Peter and John laid hands on the believers in Samaria (Philip's revival), and they received the baptism in the Holy Spirit (Acts 8:17).

13) Philip is translated by the Spirit of God to another preaching assignment (Acts 8:39-40).

14) Saul of Tarsus experienced a bright light that caused him to fall to the earth. He heard an audible voice from heaven. He is struck blind for three days. During that time, he has a vision of a man named Ananias coming and putting his hands on him to receive his sight. The vision was fulfilled, so Saul (Paul) received his sight and was filled with the Holy Spirit. This is a whole series of connected supernatural events that could

only appear to be signs and wonders (Acts 9:1-18).

15) Peter was involved in healing of Aeneas who had been bedfast for eight years (Acts 9:32-35).

16) Dorcas is raised from the dead (Acts 9:36-42).

17) Peter experiences a trance and vision (Acts 10:9-19 & 11:1-18).

18) An angel appears in a vision to Cornelius giving him instructions to send for Peter. He even tells him where Peter is (Acts 10:3-6).

19) The Holy Spirit is poured out on the household of Cornelius, evidenced by them speaking in tongues, while Peter preaches to them (Acts10:44-47).

20) The angel of the Lord delivers Peter from prison again (Acts 12:1-19).

21) Herod is "smitten" by the angel of the Lord "because he gave not God the glory" and died when people called him a god. (Acts 12:23).

22) Elymas, the sorcerer, is struck blind for a season by God as either prophesied by Paul or called down on him by Paul (Acts 13:8-12).

23) In Acts 14:3 the Lord gave signs and wonders through the hands of Paul and his co-laborers to give testimony to the Word of God they preached.

24) In Acts 14:8-18 the Lord heals a crippled man through the

ministry of Paul.

25) In Acts 15:12 Paul and Barnabas recount to the church the signs and wonders the Lord had done through them among the Gentiles. The specific signs and wonders are not named.

26) In Acts 16:16-18 the Apostle Paul discerns a woman is demonic and proceeds to cast the demon out. This could be called a sign and wonder.

27) In Acts 16:26-34 a great earthquake causes the doors of the prison where Paul and Silas are incarcerated to open. Additionally, we read the chains fell off of the prisoners. The commentators almost overwhelmingly agree this was not an ordinary earthquake, but this was Divine activity. If this is so, and the reaction by the Philippian jailor suggests he saw it that way as well, then this is a sign and wonder. This would make the third time the Lord had released His people from jail.

28) In Acts 19:1-7 Paul laid hands on twelve men, all of whom received the baptism in the Spirit and spoke in tongues.

29) In this same chapter special miracles were wrought by the hands of Paul (Acts 19:11). The word for special comes from a word which contains the thought of hitting the mark. It can include the thought of pummeling or hitting one over and over again. Additionally, cloths which had touched Paul's body were laid on those who were sick or demonized, and they were healed and/or delivered (Acts 19:12).

30) Seven sons of Sceva attempted to cast out demons as they had seen Paul do and were beaten up by the demoniac (Acts 19:13-16).

31) In Acts 20:9-12 Eutychus was raised from the dead.

32) Paul perceives, which appears to be a word of knowledge, that the voyage the ship is preparing to take will be full of danger. He appears to counsel the owner of the ship not to set sail (Acts 27:10).

33) Later (vs. 23) the angel of the Lord appears to Paul to affirm to him that they will make it to shore safely. At that moment and again later Paul urges to crew to eat prophesying they will all arrive at shore safely.

34) In Acts 28 Paul feels no ill effect from the bite of a venomous snake.

35) The healing of Publius' father and the subsequent healing of many others on the island (Acts 28).

There are thirteen references to healing...deliverance...raising of dead.

There are three references to unspecified signs and wonders that probably included healing.

There are six references to people being filled with the Holy Spirit (usually speaking in tongues).

There are three or four references to Divine Judgment.

There are three references to the apostles being released supernaturally from prison.

There are two references to Jesus (resurrection and ascension).

There is one reference to supernatural transportation (other than

Jesus).

There are seven or eight references to trances, visions, audible voices, words of knowledge, prophecy, etc.

There is one reference to Divine Protection from wild animals.

Finally, there are four references to angels.

APPENDIX TWO
Ministry Team Guidelines

1. All ministry team members must be actively involved in the pre-service prayer meetings. Only those who attend meetings will receive a ministry name tag, and ONLY those wearing a ministry name tag will be released to pray.

2. Listen to any instructions given during the meeting and work as instructed

3. All ministry team members must be in the auditorium for the altar call, and ready to move quickly to people needing ministry at the instruction of those leading the meeting.

4. Be sensitive at all times - Is the person comfortable with you praying for them? Ask the person their name and what area of need they have come for. Make them feel at ease. The person you are praying for needs to be assured that he/she is the most important person at that moment. Don't become distracted, looking at others or around the room while ministering to the person in front of you.

5. Be sensitive in the area of physical contact. Touching the hands, arm, shoulders, or head is appropriate.

6. Good personal hygiene is essential - Have clean teeth, use deodorant, perfume and breath fresheners at all times.

7. Ensure your support person ministers with you as you minister, and catches as necessary

8. When deliverance or deep ministry is taking place, wisdom and discretion are to be used in the situation. If manifestations become noisy, check with the ministry coordinator before continuing.

9. You may be required to counsel for salvation or personal situations. The prayer room can be used if counseling necessary, but speak to the coordinator first.

10. Make sure everyone who is on the altar call has been ministered to before you leave.

11. If in doubt in a situation ask for advice from a ministry team coordinator

12. Please work on maintaining a close relationship with the Lord both before and during conference week, and actively seek his anointing on your life and ministry.

Thank you all for making yourself available to serve in this way. We appreciate all you do and are going to do.

APPENDIX THREE
Ministry Team Guidelines – Catchers

1. Wait until you are called up after the altar call, stand with your altar ministry workers and wait until instructions are given before you begin talking to them. Look for an open area before you begin to pray; this will avoid falling on others.

2. The altar ministry worker will remain in close interaction with the person, ready to pray a personal prayer and blessing for the individual at this time. Keep your eyes open at all times and watch the person you are catching at all times. Don't be looking around at others!

3. You are working with the altar ministry worker as necessary. When behind the person gently touch them on the shoulders to let them know you are there in preparation to catch them. Remove your hands afterward. If the person falls, hold hands on their back just above their waist, not under the arms. Do NOT pray aloud. You may pray quietly to yourself. Hearing prayers from behind and in front will be distracting.

4. If the person requests deliverance, your altar worker will tell one of the team leaders who will notify someone on the platform, and they will handle it from there. Do not get into a discussion about it, minimize engagement in conversation.

5. Please be prepared to stay until the end of the service in your assigned position. All prayer ceases when the authorities have left.

Thank you all for making yourself available to serve in this way. We really appreciate all you are going to do.

About the Author

Michael Livengood was born into the home of an Assemblies of God pastor in the state of Illinois. Prior to itinerant ministry, Michael served as a pastor for ten years in growing churches. He and his wife Linda, speaker and intercessor in her own right have traveled in itinerant ministry since 1984. Michael and Linda are the parents of two sons and six grandchildren.

Michael Livengood has been called a "Pastor's Evangelist" and a "Pastor's Pastor." He has served in numerous capacities within his denomination and in city wide Pastor's organizations. As an evangelist, he has traveled and ministered in sixteen countries, and an already effective ministry went to new dimensions after being strongly impacted by the revival at the Brownsville Assembly of God.

Over 40 of the meetings he has been invited to speak at have "broken open" into revival at some level, giving Michael a unique perspective to speak on the subject of revival and The Wow Factor. One of those churches has been in revival for more than seven years. A spin-off of that move is more than six years old. Three meetings in New Zealand ran four months or longer, with one church in a move of God that has run nearly twenty years.

To contact the author, go to his website:
www.mikelivengoodministries.com

Michael Livengood is also the author of
"The Glory Factor" © 2016
A must read on the relationship between revival
and the Glory of God!

Made in the USA
Columbia, SC
09 January 2020

86384198R00117